VEGETARIAN SLOW COOKER

LIBBY SILBERMANN

hamlyn

First published in Great Britain in 2021 by Hamlyn,
an imprint of Octopus Publishing Group Ltd
Carmelite House
50 Victoria Embankment
London EC4Y 0DZ
www.octopusbooks.co.uk

An Hachette UK Company
www.hachette.co.uk

Distributed in the US by
Hachette Book Group
1290 Avenue of the Americas
4th and 5th Floors
New York, NY 10104

Distributed in Canada by
Canadian Manda Group
664 Annette Street
Toronto, Ontario, Canada M6S 2C8

ISBN 978-0-60063-694-6

A CIP catalogue record for this book is available
from the British Library.

Printed and bound in China.

10 9 8 7 6 5 4 3 2 1

Senior Commissioning Editor: Louise McKeever
Editor: Ella Parsons
Copyeditor: Joanne Murray
Senior Designer: Jaz Bahra
Designer: Fiona Gacki
Photographer: William Shaw
Food Stylist: Libby Silbermann
Props Stylist: Jenny Iggleden
Senior Production Controller: Emily Noto

CONTENTS

Introduction 4

BREAKFASTS 8

MAINS: 3½ HOURS OR LESS 24

MAINS: MORE THAN 3½ HOURS 64

SWEET TREATS 108

Index 126

Cook's Notes 128

INTRODUCTION

A slow cooker is a brilliant alternative to oven cooking. You can leave it for many hours to cook away and do the work for you or use it as a tool to create impressive dinner party dishes. It is surprisingly versatile and often creates the optimum environment for low and slow cooking.

This book includes recipes that cover breakfast, light lunches, long and slow dinners and sweet-treat desserts – all updated and adapted to use the best vegetarian ingredients available.

Although the slow cooker will do the majority (if not all) of the work in most of these recipes, some recipes involve some extra steps for maximum flavour, such as frying, sautéing, roasting or grilling. Similarly, some dishes require finishing in the oven or under the grill.

Slow cookers are increasing in popularity and, despite their association with slow-cooking meat, the recipes in this book will demonstrate the wide spectrum of vegetarian dishes that are possible in your slow cooker. I hope it fills you with inspiration at the endless possibilities of wonderful, delicious and highly varied vegetarian dishes you can create in your slow cooker.

A note on slow cooker capacity
All the recipes in this book were tested in a 6.5 litre (11½ pint) slow cooker, so adjust quantities and cooking times according to the capacity of your slow cooker if necessary. Take particular care with baking recipes.

SLOW COOKER TOP TIPS

Follow these simple guidelines to ensure successful slow cooking every time.

Less is more

If you're adapting one of your favourite recipes to be made in the slow cooker, be sure to reduce the liquid content by at least one-third, if not one-half. Because of the tight-fitting lid and prolonged cooking process, most of the liquid will not evaporate from a slow cooker, so you could end up with a thin, runny sauce. If this does happen, transfer the cooking liquid to a saucepan and simmer briskly, uncovered, on the hob until reduced, or remove 2 tablespoons of the cooking liquid and mix with 1 tablespoon of cornflour in a cup until smooth, return to the pan and simmer for a few minutes, stirring, until thickened.

Layer flavours

Although a lot of the time it can be tempting to skip preliminary stages like sautéeing onions and garlic, toasting spices or marinating vegetables, these steps will add deep flavour to your dishes. You can, of course, just throw all the ingredients into the slow cooker to cook, but you might end up with something a little less tasty.

Consider temperature

Be mindful of whether your ingredients are fridge-cold before going into the slow cooker – this will affect cooking times. Make sure any stock in the recipe is boiling hot before it's added or this will delay the cooking process. If you're in a hurry, preheat your slow cooker while you prep.

Keep greens fresh

Slow cooking some green vegetables can lead to them looking a bit brown and sludgy. Unless otherwise instructed, always add leafy green vegetables and fresh herbs at the last minute to keep things vibrant.

Put a lid on it (sometimes)

We always want to peek into our slow cooker to check on progress, but it's important to resist the urge, as opening the lid lets the carefully calibrated temperature of the slow cooker dip and can affect your dish. Each time you open the lid will add about 15 minutes to the cooking time. However, when baking certain dishes or attempting to reduce liquid in a dish, it's often advisable to place a tea towel or kitchen paper underneath the lid to trap the steam, or to position the lid slightly ajar for some of the cooking time to allow steam to escape, as directed where appropriate in the recipes.

Make cleaning up a breeze

Where possible, grease your slow cooker pot to avoid any stuck-on food at the end of the cooking process. When baking or cooking a very sticky mixture, line the pot with nonstick baking paper, or stock up on specially designed plastic slow cooker liners that can prevent burnt bottoms and crusty slow cooker pots.

Be flexible

Slow cooking is not the most intuitive way to cook and different models of slow cooker run at slightly different temperatures, so you have to keep a degree of flexibility with cooking times and get to know your own cooker. A recipe that says it takes 2 hours to cook could be ready in closer to half that time in some slow cookers.

Highs and lows

Most slow cookers have two functions: 'high' and 'low'. If you want to cook something for longer than stated, or need it on the table sooner, as a general rule of thumb it takes twice as long to cook something on low than on high. For example, if a recipe states 8 hours on low, you could cook it for 4 hours on high instead. It is also worth noting that power and temperature settings vary with different brands of slow cookers. Therefore, although all the cook times are accurate for the recipes in this book, it is worth checking your dishes from time to time as they cook.

Reheating and storing

Don't use your ceramic slow cooker pot to store leftovers, as it's designed to keep the contents warm for extended periods of time and can lead to harmful bacteria breeding. Similarly, do not use your slow cooker to reheat leftovers, as harmful bacteria can reproduce in the time it takes for the pot to heat up.

Prep like a pro

When preparing your ingredients, think carefully about the size you are cutting your vegetables into. Are you cooking on low for 10 hours? Make the pieces bigger so that they don't turn into mush. Need dinner on the table in an hour? Cut them as small as you can to ensure even cooking in a short space of time. Plan ahead certain recipes that you can prep for in advance – any that call for all ingredients just to be dropped into the slow cooker can be chopped and prepared, frozen in freezer bags, defrosted and then cooked straight away.

Timing is everything

A lot of slow cookers don't have built-in timers, so make sure you have one nearby for setting the cooking time – you could attach a kitchen timer to the lid of your slow cooker – because it's very easy to lose track of whatever you're cooking and ruin dinner!

Stay steady and safe

Make sure your slow cooker is on a secure flat surface away from anything flammable or delicate – the outside of the cooker can get very hot, so you need to be careful when handling it.

VEGETARIAN INGREDIENTS

While you're probably well versed in buying vegetarian produce, here is a list of ingredients that can sometimes contain meat. Always make sure you double check the food label on the packaging before purchasing. There are, of course, vegetarian alternatives to all the following items, so you shouldn't run into any difficulty, but it's important to keep these in mind when shopping.

Cheese

Some traditional cheesemaking processes use animal rennet, which makes the product non-vegetarian. Make sure you buy cheese made with vegetarian rennet instead.

Pesto

Pesto often contains Parmesan cheese, which is made with animal rennet.

Wine

Wine can contain animal proteins that are used in the fermentation, clarifying and fining processes, so always double check the label.

Worcestershire sauce

Non-vegetarian Worcestershire sauce traditionally contains anchovies.

Vinegar

Vinegar can contain animal proteins. Vegetarian vinegars are available but always double check the label. Alternatively, all distilled vinegars and malt vinegars are vegetarian, and acidic flavours such as lemon juice can also be used in their place.

BREAKFASTS

Cooking your porridge slowly results in a creamy-tasting porridge, plus no stirring is required. The basic recipe is made with oats and full-fat or coconut milk, but you can experiment with different non-dairy milks, stir through dried fruit, or even add grated chocolate for a more decadent breakfast.

SERVES 4 • PREPARATION TIME 5 MINUTES • COOKING TIME 4 HOURS

SLOW COOKER CREAMY PORRIDGE

100 g (3½ oz) jumbo oats
500 ml (17 fl oz) milk or
    400 ml (14 fl oz) can coconut
    milk mixed with 100 ml
    (3½ fl oz) water
1 teaspoon ground cinnamon
    (optional)
handful of dried fruit (optional)
100 g (3½ oz) plain dark
    chocolate, grated (optional)

Put the oats and milk into the slow cooker and stir well. Add the cinnamon, dried fruits or chocolate, if using, cover with the lid and cook on low for 4 hours until the porridge has reached your desired consistency.

Serve just as it is or with your choice of topping – try a drizzle of clear honey and sliced banana, fresh berries, Raspberry Chia Seed Jam (see page 16), Fruit Compote (see page 17), toasted coconut flakes and mango slices, or cacao nibs and nut butter.

Turmeric has numerous health benefits, in particular its anti-inflammatory properties, which can help digestion and bloating. This golden milk is a wonderful way to start the day and is incredibly comforting, with warm and fragrant cinnamon and cardamom.

SERVES 2 • PREPARATION TIME 5 MINUTES • COOKING TIME 2 HOURS

GOLDEN TURMERIC MILK

500 ml (17 fl oz) dairy-free milk, such as almond, oat or coconut
1 teaspoon turmeric
½ teaspoon ground ginger
1 cinnamon stick
pinch of black pepper
pinch of ground cardamom
2 tablespoons maple syrup, honey or agave syrup

ground cinnamon, to serve (optional)

Put all the ingredients into the slow cooker and whisk well until completely combined. Cover with the lid and cook on low for 2 hours.

Ladle the warm milk into mugs and serve immediately, dusted with a little ground cinnamon, if liked. Alternatively, froth the milk with a milk frother before serving.

The low and consistent temperatures of a slow cooker make it the perfect environment to culture yogurt. This recipe does take a little culturing time, but the resulting yogurt is so versatile (and full of gut-loving live cultures) and you can use a portion of it as the starter for your next batch.

MAKES 2 KG (4 LB) • PREPARATION TIME 5 MINUTES, PLUS STANDING AND FERMENTING COOKING TIME 2½ HOURS

BIO-CULTURED YOGURT

2 litres (3½ pints) milk
100 g (3½ oz) natural live yogurt (check the packaging for live cultures)
vanilla bean paste or honey (optional)

blackberries, blueberries and halved cherries, to serve (optional)

Pour the milk into the slow cooker, cover with the lid and cook on low for 2½ hours. Turn off the cooker and leave to stand with the lid on for 3 hours.

Ladle 500 ml (17 fl oz) of the warm milk into a large bowl, add the yogurt and whisk together until smooth. Return the mixture to the slow cooker and stir well, then replace the lid. Wrap the slow cooker in a large towel so it is well insulated (this creates a good environment for the yogurt cultures to become active). Leave to ferment, without lifting the lid, for 8 hours until set and ready to use.

Transfer to an airtight container and store in the refrigerator for up to 2 weeks. To continue culturing your own yogurt, reserve 100 ml (3½ fl oz) from this batch to use as your starter for the next.

Mix the yogurt with a little vanilla bean paste or honey, if liked, before serving with blackberries, blueberries and halved cherries, or you could try other chopped fruit, such as mango, peach, raspberries or banana. This yogurt is also delicious served on Honey, Nut & Seed Granola (see page 14) or in little pots on top of Raspberry Chia Seed Jam (see page 16) or Fruit Compote (see page 17).

This recipe is brilliant for making and storing a large batch of granola. The nuts, seeds and dried fruit are easily interchangeable, so experiment and try different flavour combinations.

**MAKES 12 SERVINGS • PREPARATION TIME 10 MINUTES, PLUS COOLING
COOKING TIME 2½ HOURS**

HONEY, NUT & SEED GRANOLA

350 g (11½ oz) jumbo oats
100 g (3½ oz) coconut flakes
50 g (2 oz) sunflower seeds
50 g (2 oz) raw almonds,
    chopped
50 g (2 oz) walnuts, chopped
1 teaspoon ground cinnamon
4 tablespoons coconut oil,
    melted
175 g (6 oz) clear honey
    or agave syrup
50 ml (2 fl oz) water
1 teaspoon vanilla extract
125 g (4 oz) raisins
50 g (2 oz) dried cranberries

TO SERVE
shop-bought yogurt or
    homemade yogurt
    (see page 13)
fresh berries

Put the oats, coconut flakes, seeds, nuts and cinnamon into the slow cooker and mix well.

Mix together the coconut oil, honey or agave syrup, measured water and vanilla extract in a small bowl, then pour this over the oat mixture and stir until well combined.

Cover with the lid at a slight angle so there is a small gap to allow the steam to escape (this will help the granola to crisp), then cook on high for 2½ hours, stirring gently every 40 minutes to ensure the mixture is not sticking to the pot or burning.

Carefully remove the slow cooker pot from the cooker using oven gloves, then carefully tip the granola onto a large baking tray and spread it out evenly. Leave to cool (this ensures it will be crunchy), then stir in the raisins and cranberries. Store in an airtight container for up to 2 weeks.

Serve the granola with yogurt and fresh berries, or simply with your milk of choice.

This raspberry jam is incredibly easy to make and uses dates as a sweetener, which makes it much healthier than many supermarket jams. Keep it in the refrigerator for up to two weeks and bring it out at breakfast time.

MAKES 2 x 375 G (12 OZ) JAR • PREPARATION TIME 15 MINUTES, PLUS COOLING & OVERNIGHT SETTING • COOKING TIME 3 HOURS

RASPBERRY CHIA SEED JAM

625 g (1¼ lb) raspberries
4 teaspoons chia seeds
10 dates, pitted and chopped

Put all the ingredients into the slow cooker, cover with the lid and cook on low for 3 hours until the fruit and dates have completely softened.

Mash the mixture in the slow cooker pot with a fork or potato masher until it reaches your desired consistency (bear in mind that the jam will thicken as it cools). Alternatively, for a smoother jam, carefully transfer the mixture to a blender and blend to a smooth purée. Leave to cool.

Preheat the oven to 180°C (350°F), Gas Mark 4. Put 2 x 375 g (12 oz) clean jars in the oven for 15 minutes to sterilize. Spoon the cooled jam into the sterilized jars and seal, then place in the refrigerator to thicken and set overnight. If the jam is added when the jars are still warm (and the jam is also warm), they will need to cool to room temperature first. Store in the refrigerator for up to 2 weeks.

Serve the jam spread over warm toast or dolloped on to yogurt (see page 13) or porridge (see page 10).

This stewed fruit recipe is delicious and so versatile – you can replace the plums with other fruit that you like or that are in season or available, such as apples, pears, rhubarb and apricots, which all work well. Simply adjust the sugar to taste depending on the tartness of the fruit.

SERVES 4–6 • PREPARATION TIME 10 MINUTES • COOKING TIME 3 HOURS

FRUIT COMPOTE

12 plums, about 1.25 kg (2½ lb) in total, halved and stoned
200 g (7 oz) golden caster sugar
1 cinnamon stick or ½ teaspoon ground cinnamon
½ teaspoon vanilla bean paste
100 ml (3½ fl oz) water

Put all the ingredients into the slow cooker and mix together until the plums are well coated. Cover with a lid and cook on low for 3 hours until the plums are soft and the juices thickened.

Serve warm or cold, with thick, creamy yogurt (see page 13) or stirred through porridge (see page 10). The compote can also be served on its own as a dessert.

French toast is a great weekend treat. This cinnamon-spiced version with blueberries is delicious served warm and drizzled with honey, alongside thick Greek yogurt and plenty of coffee.

SERVES 4 • PREPARATION TIME 15 MINUTES, PLUS OVERNIGHT SOAKING COOKING TIME 4 HOURS

BLUEBERRY & CINNAMON FRENCH TOAST

50 g (2 oz) butter, softened, plus extra for greasing
1 teaspoon ground cinnamon
150 g (5 oz) soft brown sugar, plus extra for sprinkling
8 slices of bread, slightly stale
1 teaspoon vanilla bean paste
pinch of sea salt
3 large eggs
300 ml (½ pint) milk
100 g (3½ oz) blueberries, plus extra to serve

TO SERVE
natural Greek yogurt
clear honey

Beat together the butter, cinnamon and sugar in a small bowl until it forms a smooth paste, then carefully spread each slice of bread with the butter mixture on both sides.

Whisk together the vanilla bean paste, salt, eggs and milk in a large, shallow dish until smooth. Place the slices of bread into the egg mixture, ensuring each slice is submerged. Cover the dish with clingfilm and place in the refrigerator overnight.

When ready to cook, grease the slow cooker pot well with butter. Arrange a layer of the soaked bread slices in the bottom of the pot. Sprinkle over a layer of blueberries, then add another layer of bread. Repeat until all the bread and blueberries are used, then pour over any remaining egg mixture and sprinkle the top with sugar.

Cover with the lid and cook on low for 4 hours until the egg mixture has thickened and set. Carefully remove the slow cooker pot from the cooker using oven gloves. Cut the French toast into slices and serve with dollops of Greek yogurt, extra blueberries and a drizzle of clear honey.

A frittata is a great brunch option for entertaining. Cooked directly in the slow cooker pot, this recipe is brilliantly simple and delicious. Serve warm or chill in the refrigerator, to serve cold for lunch another day.

SERVES 4 • PREPARATION TIME 45 MINUTES • COOKING TIME 2 HOURS

SWEET POTATO, GOATS' CHEESE & THYME FRITTATA

2 sweet potatoes, about 625 g (1¼ lb) in total, peeled and cut into bite-sized pieces

2 tablespoons olive oil, plus extra for greasing

1 onion, finely sliced

3 garlic cloves, finely sliced

6 large eggs

1 tablespoon thyme, leaves picked

50 g (2 oz) soft goats' cheese

salt and pepper

Preheat the oven to 200°C (400°F), Gas Mark 6. Put the sweet potatoes on a baking tray. Drizzle with 1 tablespoon of the oil, then season well with salt and pepper and toss until well coated. Roast for 25–30 minutes until tender and lightly golden brown.

Meanwhile, heat the remaining oil in a frying pan, add the onion and fry over a medium-low heat for 5 minutes until soft and translucent, then stir in the garlic and cook for 3 minutes until the onion and garlic are lightly golden.

Grease the slow cooker pot well with oil, then add the onion mixture and roasted sweet potatoes and mix until combined. Beat together the eggs in a large bowl. Add the thyme leaves, crumble in the goats' cheese and season well, then pour the egg mixture over the sweet potatoes.

Cover with a lid and cook on low for 2 hours until the eggs are set and a skewer inserted into the frittata comes out clean. Carefully remove the slow cooker pot from the cooker using oven gloves. Loosen the edge of the frittata with a knife and turn out onto a large plate. Cut the frittata into slices and serve warm, or store in the refrigerator for up to 3 days, to serve cold on another occasion.

This is an exciting alternative to the usual eggs on toast, bursting with Middle Eastern spices. The long cooking time allows the sauce to thicken and develop in flavour. You can make it vegan by omitting the eggs and using vegan cheese and yogurt.

SERVES 4 · PREPARATION TIME 10 MINUTES · COOKING TIME 5 HOURS 20 MINUTES

SHAKSHUKA

1 onion, finely sliced
3 garlic cloves, crushed
460 g (14¾ oz) jar roasted red peppers, drained and sliced
300 g (10 oz) mixed-colour cherry tomatoes, chopped
2 x 400 g (13 oz) cans chopped tomatoes
2 tablespoons tomato purée
1 teaspoon smoked paprika
1 teaspoon ground cumin
1 teaspoon dried oregano
4 large eggs
50 g (2 oz) feta cheese
10 g (¼ oz) coriander, chopped, to garnish

TO SERVE
pitta breads or flatbreads
natural yogurt

Put the onion, garlic, red peppers, fresh and canned tomatoes, tomato purée, paprika, cumin and oregano into the slow cooker and mix together. Cover with the lid and cook on low for 5 hours until tender and full of flavour.

Make 4 wells in the surface of the mixture, then carefully crack an egg into each well and crumble over the feta cheese. Replace the lid and cook on high for about 15–20 minutes until the egg whites are set but the yolks are still runny.

Meanwhile, toast the pitta breads or flatbreads, or warm them through in a preheated oven according to the packet instructions.

Divide the eggs and tomato mixture among 4 serving dishes and sprinkle with the chopped coriander. Serve with dollops of yogurt and the toasted pitta breads or flatbreads.

These smoky beans are a healthier, and more flavoursome, alternative to baked beans. Serve them simply piled on buttered toast or alongside vegetarian sausages, grilled tomatoes and poached eggs for a vegetarian version of a full cooked breakfast.

SERVES 4 · PREPARATION TIME 15 MINUTES · COOKING TIME 5 HOURS

SMOKY BREAKFAST BEANS

1 tablespoon olive oil

1 onion, finely sliced

3 garlic cloves, crushed

400 g (13 oz) can haricot beans, drained

300 g (10 oz) passata (sieved tomatoes)

1 tablespoon tomato purée

1 bay leaf

20 g (¾ oz) soft brown sugar

1 teaspoon smoked paprika

1 tablespoon apple cider vinegar

handful of parsley, chopped, to garnish

buttered toast, to serve

Heat the oil in a frying pan, add the onion and fry over a medium-low heat for 5 minutes until soft and translucent, then stir in the garlic and fry for 3 minutes until the onion and garlic are lightly golden.

Transfer the onion mixture to the slow cooker, then add the remaining ingredients and mix together until well combined. Cover with the lid and cook on low for 5 hours until the sauce has thickened and the beans are soft. Alternatively, cook on high for 3 hours.

Serve the beans piled on to buttered toast, sprinkled with the chopped parsley.

MAINS:
3½ HOURS OR LESS

This hearty risotto is made more rustic with the use of pearl barley and is packed with earthy umami flavours from the miso.

SERVES 4 • PREPARATION TIME 20 MINUTES • COOKING TIME 2½ HOURS

MUSHROOM PEARL BARLEY RISOTTO

2 tablespoons olive oil, plus extra
 to serve

1 onion, finely chopped

1 leek, trimmed, cleaned and
 finely chopped

4 garlic cloves, crushed

100 g (3½ oz) chestnut
 mushrooms, chopped

100 g (3½ oz) shiitake
 mushrooms, sliced

250 g (8 oz) pearl barley

1.5 litres (2½ pints) mushroom
 or vegetable stock

1 tablespoon white miso paste

small handful of thyme sprigs,
 leaves picked, plus extra leaves
 to garnish

100 g (3½ oz) crème fraîche

100 g (3½ oz) vegetarian Italian
 hard cheese, finely grated,
 plus extra to serve

salt and pepper

GARLIC MUSHROOMS

1 tablespoon olive oil

75 g (3 oz) shiitake mushrooms,
 sliced

3 garlic cloves, crushed

1 tablespoon unsalted butter

salt and pepper

Heat the oil in a large frying pan, add the onion and leek and fry over a medium-low heat for about 5 minutes until soft and the onion is translucent. Stir in the garlic and fry for a few minutes until softened. Add the mushrooms and fry for a further 3–4 minutes until just tender and beginning to turn golden.

Transfer the mushroom mixture to the slow cooker and add the pearl barley, stock, miso paste and thyme. Cover with the lid and cook on high for 2½ hours until the barley is tender and the sauce thickened. Stir through the crème fraîche and cheese and season to taste with salt and pepper.

Cook the garlic-fried mushrooms 10 minutes before the end of the risotto cooking time. Heat the oil in a large frying pan and add the sliced mushrooms. Fry over a medium-low heat for 3 minutes until beginning to soften. Add the crushed garlic and continue to fry for 2 minutes until the mushrooms are golden brown. Add the butter to the pan and toss to coat the mushrooms. Season with salt and pepper.

Spoon the risotto into serving bowls, then sprinkle with thyme leaves and drizzle with good-quality olive oil. Serve with extra grated cheese and the garlic-fried mushrooms.

You will need to do some prep for this one (you might want to wear gloves when you peel the beetroot to avoid staining your hands), but trust me, it is well worth the little bit of extra effort.

SERVES 6 • PREPARATION TIME 55 MINUTES • COOKING TIME 2 HOURS

BEETROOT RISOTTO WITH STILTON & WALNUTS

400 g (13 oz) fresh beetroot, peeled and chopped into 3 cm (1¼ inch) cubes
2 tablespoons olive oil
1 teaspoon fennel seeds
100 ml (3½ fl oz) water
1 onion, finely chopped
2 garlic cloves, crushed
250 g (8 oz) arborio rice
200 ml (7 fl oz) red wine
1 litre (1¾ pints) vegetable stock
100 g (3½ oz) walnuts
50 g (2 oz) butter
100 g (3½ oz) Stilton or other hard blue cheese, rind removed
salt and pepper
small handful of dill fronds, to garnish

Preheat the oven to 180°C (350°F), Gas Mark 4. Put the beetroot on a baking tray. Drizzle with 1 tablespoon of the oil, sprinkle with the fennel seeds and season with salt and pepper. Toss until coated. Roast for 40 minutes until tender. Leave to cool slightly, then tip two-thirds of the beetroot into a food processor or blender, pour in the measured water and blitz to a purée. Set aside the remaining beetroot.

Meanwhile, heat the remaining oil in a frying pan, add the onion and fry over a medium-low heat for 5 minutes until soft and translucent, then stir in the garlic and fry for a few minutes until softened. Add the rice and cook for a further few minutes, stirring until well coated in the onion mixture and the rice makes a light popping sound. Pour in the wine and bring to the boil, then bubble until reduced by half.

Transfer the rice mixture to the slow cooker, add the beetroot purée and stock and season well. Cover with the lid and cook on low for 2 hours until the rice is tender and the sauce thickened and glossy.

Meanwhile, heat a large, dry frying pan over a medium-low heat, add the walnuts and toast for 5 minutes, stirring frequently, until golden brown. Leave to cool, then roughly chop. Set aside.

When the risotto is cooked, add the butter and stir through until melted, then stir in the reserved beetroot. Adjust the seasoning to taste. Spoon into bowls, crumble over the blue cheese and top with the toasted walnuts. Serve sprinkled with the dill fronds.

This is a bright and summery risotto, with the fresh flavours of lemon and spring vegetables. Perfect for entertaining guests.

SERVES 4 • PREPARATION TIME 25 MINUTES, PLUS STANDING • COOKING TIME 1 HOUR

SUMMERY PEA, ASPARAGUS & LEMON RISOTTO

1 tablespoon butter, plus extra to serve

1 tablespoon olive oil, plus extra to serve

1 onion, finely chopped

1 leek, trimmed, cleaned and finely chopped

2 garlic cloves, crushed

350 g (11½ oz) arborio rice

200 ml (7 fl oz) white wine

1 litre (1¾ pints) vegetable stock

100 g (3½ oz) vegetarian Italian hard cheese, grated, plus extra shavings to serve

grated zest of 1 unwaxed lemon

200 g (7 oz) frozen peas

100 g (3½ oz) fine asparagus, cut into 3 cm (1¼ inch) pieces

2 tablespoons chopped parsley

100 g (3½ oz) wild rocket

salt and pepper

Heat the butter and oil in a large frying pan, add the onion and leek and fry over a medium-low heat for about 5 minutes until soft and the onion is translucent, then stir in the garlic and fry for a few minutes until softened. Add the rice and cook for a further few minutes, stirring until well coated in the onion mixture and the rice makes a light popping sound. Pour in the wine and cook until the alcohol has evaporated and the liquid has been absorbed.

Transfer the rice mixture to the slow cooker and pour in the stock. Cover with the lid and cook on high for 1 hour until the rice is just tender and the liquid has been absorbed.

Turn off the slow cooker, then add the cheese, lemon zest, frozen peas, asparagus, parsley and most of the rocket and stir well. Replace the lid and leave to stand for 5–10 minutes until the asparagus is tender. Add a knob of butter and stir through until melted. Season well with salt and pepper.

Spoon into shallow bowls and serve with a drizzle of olive oil, the remaining rocket and some cheese shavings.

Apple and parsnip make a brilliant pairing, with coconut cream making the soup creamy and silky. Served with delicious, crunchy, rustic croutons, this is the ultimate comfort food.

SERVES 4 • PREPARATION TIME 10 MINUTES • COOKING TIME 3 HOURS 10 MINUTES

PARSNIP & APPLE SOUP

5 parsnips, about 500 g (1 lb) in total, roughly chopped
1 onion, roughly chopped
1 cooking apple or 2 tart dessert apples, about 250 g (8 oz) in total, peeled, cored and roughly chopped
1 teaspoon turmeric
1.5 litres (2½ pints) vegetable stock
50 ml (2 fl oz) coconut cream
salt and pepper

croutons, to serve (optional)

Put all the ingredients except the coconut cream into the slow cooker, cover with the lid and cook on high for 3 hours until the vegetables and apples are tender and soft.

Turn off the slow cooker and leave to cool slightly, then purée the soup while still in the slow cooker pot using a stick blender. Alternatively, carefully transfer the soup to a blender and blend, in batches if necessary, until smooth, then return to the slow cooker. Cook the soup on high for a further 10 minutes, to warm through.

Stir through the coconut cream, then season to taste with salt and add a good grinding of pepper.

Ladle into bowls and serve topped with crunchy croutons, if liked.

The combination of pea and watercress is classic for a reason. The peppery and fresh flavour makes it a brilliant light starter or lunch option. Make the soup in advance (it will keep in the refrigerator for up to 5 days) and simply reheat before serving.

SERVES 4 • PREPARATION TIME 25 MINUTES • COOKING TIME 3 HOURS

PEA & WATERCRESS SOUP

1 tablespoon olive oil

1 onion, chopped

2 celery sticks, chopped

3 garlic cloves, chopped

1 large potato, peeled and chopped

1 litre (1¾ pints) vegetable stock

400 g (13 oz) frozen peas

200 g (7 oz) watercress

salt and pepper

TO SERVE

100 g (3½ oz) crème fraiche

small handful of cooked peas (optional)

small handful of pea shoots (optional)

Heat the oil in a frying pan, add the onion and celery and fry over a medium heat for 5 minutes until softened, then stir in the garlic and fry for 3 minutes until softened.

Transfer the onion mixture to the slow cooker, add the potato and pour in the stock. Cover with the lid and cook on high for 2½ hours.

Stir in the frozen peas and watercress, replace the lid and cook, still on high, for a further 20 minutes until the vegetables are tender and cooked through.

Turn off the slow cooker and leave to cool slightly, then purée the soup while still in the slow cooker pot using a stick blender. Alternatively, carefully transfer the soup to a blender and blend, in batches if necessary, until smooth, then return to the slow cooker.

Season to taste with salt and pepper. Cook the soup on high for a further 10 minutes, to warm through.

Ladle into bowls and top with swirls of the crème fraiche, a good grinding of pepper and a few cooked peas and pea shoot sprigs, if liked.

This soup is full of flavour with a little hint of spice and is a great way of using the best of the winter months' vegetables. The seed topping adds crunch to the silky-smooth soup and works well with many different soups and salads.

SERVES 4–6 • PREPARATION TIME 15 MINUTES • COOKING TIME 3 HOURS 10 MINUTES

BUTTERNUT SQUASH, CARROT & FENNEL SOUP

1 butternut squash, peeled, deseeded and chopped, about 500 g (1 lb) prepared weight
650 g (1 lb 7 oz) carrots, roughly chopped
1 fennel bulb, trimmed and sliced
1 litre (1¾ pints) vegetable stock
1 teaspoon curry powder
½ teaspoon ground cumin
½ teaspoon ground cinnamon
½ teaspoon fennel seeds
½ teaspoon dried chilli flakes

CRUNCHY SEED TOPPING (OPTIONAL)
50 g (2 oz) pumpkin seeds
50 g (2 oz) sunflower seeds
50 g (2 oz) linseeds
1 tablespoon poppy seeds
1 tablespoon olive oil
½ teaspoon smoked paprika
½ teaspoon garlic granules
½ teaspoon dried rosemary

Put all the soup ingredients into the slow cooker, cover with the lid and cook on high for 3 hours until the vegetables are tender and cooked through.

Meanwhile, make the seed topping, if using. Preheat the oven to 180°C (350°F), Gas Mark 4. Mix together all the ingredients in a bowl until the seeds are well coated in the oil, then spread evenly on a baking sheet lined with greaseproof paper. Place in the oven for about 10 minutes until golden. Remove and leave to cool. Keep to one side what you want to use for the soup and store any remaining seed topping in an airtight container in a cool, dark place for up to 4 weeks.

Turn off the slow cooker and leave the soup to cool slightly, then purée while still in the slow cooker pot using a stick blender. Alternatively, carefully transfer the soup to a blender and blend, in batches if necessary, until smooth, then return to the slow cooker.

Season to taste with salt and pepper. Cook the soup on high for a further 10 minutes, to warm through.

Ladle into bowls and serve topped with a sprinkling of the crunchy seeds, if liked. You could add a little chopped parsley as well for a splash of vibrant colour.

This focaccia is simple to make and looks impressive. Once you're confident with the recipe, try mixing up the flavours.

**SERVES 6 • PREPARATION TIME 25 MINUTES, PLUS STANDING
COOKING TIME 2 HOURS 50 MINUTES**

TOMATO & ROSEMARY FOCACCIA

300 ml (½ pint) lukewarm water

1 teaspoon caster sugar

7 g (about 2 teaspoons) packet
    fast-action dried yeast

3 tablespoons olive oil, plus
    1 teaspoon for drizzling

1 teaspoon salt, plus extra
    for sprinkling

20 g (¾ oz) rosemary, leaves
    picked and chopped

500 g (1 lb) plain flour, plus
    extra for dusting

9 or 10 mixed-colour cherry
    tomatoes, halved

PESTO TOPPING

50 g (2 oz) pine nuts, toasted

100 g (3½ oz) basil leaves

2 garlic cloves

50 g (2 oz) vegetarian Italian
    hard cheese, grated

150 ml (¼ pint) extra virgin
    olive oil

salt and pepper

Put the measured water and sugar into a large bowl and stir together until slightly dissolved. Sprinkle the yeast over the surface and whisk in. Leave to stand for 15 minutes until the surface is bubbly and frothy.

Add the olive oil, salt and 3 tablespoons of the rosemary and mix well, then gradually add the flour, mixing well between each addition, until all the flour is combined. Turn the dough out on to a lightly floured surface and knead for about 10 minutes until smooth and springy.

Line the bottom and sides of the slow cooker pot with a large sheet of baking paper, then place the dough in the middle. Place a clean tea towel over the top, then cover with the lid. Turn the slow cooker setting to warm and leave the dough to rise for 30 minutes until it has doubled in size.

Remove the dough from the pot. On a lightly floured surface, knead the dough for a few minutes. Shape it into a smooth, flat ball and return to the pot. Push the tomatoes into the top, sprinkle over the remaining rosemary and a pinch of salt, then drizzle over a little olive oil. Re-cover with the tea towel and lid and leave to rise for 20 minutes until doubled in size again.

Turn the slow cooker setting to high and cook the bread for 2 hours until golden brown with a crisp crust. Carefully remove from the slow cooker and leave to cool slightly on a wire rack.

Meanwhile, make the pesto. Place all the ingredients in a food processor and gently pulse until smooth. Season with salt and pepper.

Serve the focaccia slightly warm, drizzled with the pesto.

This cornbread has a great warmth from the chilli. It is very easy to make and is perfect served with soups or alongside salads.

SERVES 6 · PREPARATION TIME 15 MINUTES · COOKING TIME 1½ HOURS

CHILLI, CHEESE & CHIVE CORNBREAD

butter, for greasing
200 g (7 oz) coarse polenta
150 g (5 oz) plain flour
2 teaspoons baking powder
1 teaspoon bicarbonate of soda
½ teaspoon smoked paprika
100 g (3½ oz) mature Cheddar cheese, grated
1 teaspoon salt
300 ml (½ pint) buttermilk
2 large eggs
1 red chilli, deseeded and finely chopped
1 tablespoon chives, finely chopped
50 g (2 oz) canned sweetcorn, drained

butter, to serve

Grease the slow cooker pot well with butter, then line the bottom and sides with baking paper.

Mix together the polenta, flour, baking powder, bicarbonate of soda, paprika, cheese and salt in a large bowl. In a separate bowl, mix together the remaining ingredients, then pour into the polenta mixture and fold together until just incorporated, being careful not to overmix (this will make the cornbread stodgy).

Transfer the batter to the prepared slow cooker, cover with the lid and cook on high for 1½ hours, or until a skewer inserted into the cornbread comes out clean. Leave to cool slightly, then remove the slow cooker pot from the cooker using oven gloves. Carefully run a knife gently around the edge of the cornbread and tip the pot to release the bread.

Serve slightly warm, spread with butter, or leave to cool completely, then freeze for up to 3 months. When you want to eat it, defrost the loaf fully, then preheat the oven to 180°C (350°F), Gas Mark 4. Wrap the cornbread in foil and place in the oven for 20 minutes until warmed through. If you froze the cornbread sliced, then you can pop the slices into the toaster from frozen.

Polenta is a grain similar to cornmeal, from Northern Italy. This creamy and cheesy recipe is brilliant served alongside a variety of dishes.

SERVES 4 • PREPARATION TIME 5 MINUTES • COOKING TIME 2½ HOURS

CREAMY CHEESY POLENTA

160 g (5½ oz) polenta
750 ml (1¼ pints) vegetable stock
½ teaspoon salt
250 ml (8 fl oz) milk
50 g (2 oz) vegetarian Italian hard
    cheese, grated
50 g (2 oz) butter, cubed
small handful of thyme sprigs,
    leaves picked, to garnish

Put the polenta, stock and salt into the slow cooker and mix together. Cover with the lid and cook on low for 2 hours.

Stir in the milk, replace the lid and cook on high for a further 30 minutes until thickened to the consistency of double cream. Add the cheese and butter and stir through until melted.

Garnish with the thyme and serve. Try topping it with garlic mushrooms (see page 26), Creamy Wild Mushroom Stroganoff (see page 84) or Mushroom Bolognese (see page 70).

You can't beat a creamy and comforting mac and cheese – and this recipe is no exception. The leeks add sweetness and Emmental is a fantastic, mildly nutty Swiss cheese. The whole dish can be prepared the day before and chilled until ready to bake.

SERVES 4 • PREPARATION TIME 15 MINUTES • COOKING TIME 2½ HOURS

MAC & CHEESE WITH LEEKS & CRISPY BREADCRUMB TOPPING

50 g (2 oz) cream cheese

500 ml (17 fl oz) milk

25 g (1 oz) butter, melted

100 g (3½ oz) Cheddar cheese, grated

100 g (3½ oz) Emmental cheese, grated

50 g (2 oz) vegetarian Italian hard cheese, grated

1 tablespoon wholegrain mustard

½ teaspoon cayenne pepper

2 garlic cloves, crushed

250 g (8 oz) dried macaroni (curved elbow macaroni, if possible)

1 leek, trimmed, cleaned and finely chopped

salt and pepper

1 tablespoon finely chopped chives, to garnish

FOR THE TOPPING

25 g (1 oz) fresh or dried panko breadcrumbs

25 g (1 oz) Emmental cheese, grated

Whisk together the cream cheese and milk in a small jug until smooth. Pour into the slow cooker, then add the melted butter, cheeses, mustard, cayenne pepper and garlic and mix together. Stir in the dried pasta and chopped leek and mix until they are well coated in the sauce.

Cover with the lid and cook on low for 2½ hours until the pasta is tender and the sauce is thick and creamy. Season to taste with salt and plenty of pepper and spoon into a 16 x 22 cm (6¼ x 8½ inch) ovenproof dish.

If making this the day before, leave to cool and then place in the refrigerator overnight. When you're ready to eat, preheat the oven to 180°C (350°F), Gas Mark 4. Remove the dish from the refrigerator, cover with foil and place in the oven for 20 minutes until warmed through. Remove the foil.

Preheat the grill. Sprinkle over the breadcrumbs and grated cheese. Place under the grill for 3 minutes until golden and the cheese has melted.

Serve immediately, sprinkled with the chives.

Cooking the orzo in with the sauce and vegetables in this dish results in a really creamy, flavoursome pasta dish, similar to a risotto. Fresh basil and plenty of Italian hard cheese perfectly finish it.

SERVES 4 • PREPARATION TIME 30 MINUTES • COOKING TIME 1 HOUR 40 MINUTES

CREAMY ORZO WITH GREEN VEG

50 g (2 oz) butter, plus extra
    to serve
2 tablespoons olive oil
1 onion, finely chopped
3 garlic cloves, crushed
150 g (5 oz) orzo pasta
200 ml (7 fl oz) white wine
500 ml (17 fl oz) vegetable stock
150 g (5 oz) frozen broad beans
100 g (3½ oz) cavolo nero, stems
    removed and leaves shredded
1 courgette, finely chopped
100 g (3½ oz) vegetarian Italian
    hard cheese, grated, plus
    extra to serve
salt and pepper
handful of basil leaves,
    to garnish

Heat the butter and oil in a large frying pan until melted and frothy. Add the onion and a pinch of salt and cook over a medium-low heat for 5 minutes until soft and translucent, then stir in the garlic and fry for a few minutes until softened. Add the orzo and cook for a further few minutes, stirring until well coated in the onion mixture and it begins to sizzle. Pour in the wine and bring to the boil, then bubble until reduced by half.

Transfer the orzo mixture to the slow cooker and pour in the stock, stirring until combined. Cover with the lid and cook on high for 1½ hours.

Stir in the frozen broad beans, cavolo nero and courgette, replace the lid and cook, still on high, for a further 10 minutes until the vegetables are tender.

When ready to serve, stack the basil leaves in a pile, then roll up and thinly slice into ribbons.

Add the cheese and a knob of butter to the cooked orzo, then stir through until melted and silky. Season to taste with salt and pepper.

Serve immediately, sprinkled with the basil and a good grating of cheese.

This recipe couldn't be easier, using store-bought tortellini. Mix up the flavours and buy any filled tortellini you like. Cooking the pasta in the sauce and topping with mozzarella results in a fantastic pasta dish that takes next to no time to prepare.

SERVES 4 • PREPARATION TIME 10 MINUTES • COOKING TIME 2 HOURS

SPINACH & RICOTTA TORTELLINI BAKE

olive oil, for greasing

2 x 300 g (10 oz) packets spinach and ricotta tortellini

750 g (1½ lb) passata (sieved tomatoes)

½ teaspoon dried chilli flakes

small handful of basil leaves, torn, plus extra to garnish

10 cherry tomatoes, halved

1 tablespoon sun-dried tomato purée

150 g (5 oz) mozzarella cheese, torn into pieces

salt and pepper

chopped parsley, to garnish

grated vegetarian Italian hard cheese, to serve

Grease the slow cooker with oil, then add all the ingredients except the mozzarella. Add half of the mozzarella, then season well with salt and pepper and mix together. Dot the remaining mozzarella over the top.

Cover with the lid and cook on high for 2 hours until the pasta is tender and the sauce thick and rich.

Garnish with chopped parsley and basil leaves and serve with grated cheese.

This take on cauliflower cheese uses both cauliflower and broccoli, to add colour and flavour. It is great served on its own but is also a fantastic comfort dish to serve alongside your Sunday lunch.

SERVES 6 • PREPARATION TIME 35 MINUTES • COOKING TIME 3 HOURS

BROCCOLI & CAULIFLOWER CHEESE

200 g (7 oz) cauliflower, cut into florets

200 g (7 oz) broccoli, cut into florets

2 x 170 g (6 oz) cans evaporated milk

200 g (7 oz) Cheddar cheese, grated

1 teaspoon wholegrain mustard

¼ nutmeg, grated

1 tablespoon chopped parsley

100 g (3½ oz) panko breadcrumbs

2 tablespoons olive oil

50 g (2 oz) vegetarian Brie, rind removed and roughly chopped

salt and pepper

steamed greens, to serve

Put the cauliflower and broccoli florets into the slow cooker. Mix together the evaporated milk, Cheddar, mustard, grated nutmeg and parsley in a bowl, then season well with salt and pepper. Pour over the vegetables and mix together until the vegetables are well coated in the sauce.

Cover with the lid and cook on low for 3 hours until the sauce is thick, the cheese melted and the vegetables tender.

Preheat the oven to 200°C (400°F), Gas Mark 6. Carefully transfer the vegetable mixture to an ovenproof dish and spread out evenly.

Mix together the panko breadcrumbs and oil in a small bowl, then season well. Dot the Brie over the vegetable mixture, then sprinkle evenly with the breadcrumbs. Bake for 10–15 minutes until the cheese has melted and the top is golden brown. Leave to stand for 5 minutes before serving with steamed greens.

The walnut and cheese crumb in this recipe makes for a flavourful gratin that works well on its own or as a Sunday lunch side dish.

SERVES 4–6 • PREPARATION TIME 1 HOUR • COOKING TIME 2 HOURS

POTATO, FENNEL & CELERIAC GRATIN

1 celeriac, about 500 g (1 lb), peeled

500 g (1 lb) floury potatoes (such as Maris Piper), peeled

1 fennel bulb, trimmed

50 g (2 oz) butter, plus extra for greasing

4 garlic cloves, finely chopped

50 g (2 oz) plain flour

1 litre (1¾ pints) milk

50 g (2 oz) Emmental cheese, grated

good grating of nutmeg

50 g (2 oz) walnuts

50 g (2 oz) fresh breadcrumbs

2 tablespoons olive oil

50 g (2 oz) vegetarian Italian hard cheese, grated

salt and pepper

steamed greens, to serve

Slice the vegetables as thinly as possible. Grease the slow cooker pot well with butter, then layer the vegetables in the pot so they are well mixed, scattering the garlic between the layers as you go.

Melt the butter in a saucepan over a medium heat, then add the flour and stir together until it resembles a sandy-coloured paste. Cook for a few minutes until it begins to smell biscuity, then pour in a small amount of the milk, remove the pan from the heat and whisk vigorously until smooth. Return the pan to the heat and continue to add the milk in small amounts, whisking until smooth after each addition, until all the milk has been added. Simmer for about 5 minutes until the sauce is smooth and thick. Add the Emmental and nutmeg, then season with salt and pepper. Continue to cook for a few minutes, stirring continuously, until the sauce is smooth.

Pour the sauce over the vegetables in the slow cooker, ensuring they are evenly covered. Cover with the lid and cook on high for 2 hours until the sauce is thickened and the vegetables are tender.

Meanwhile, put the walnuts into a food processor and pulse until they resemble fine crumbs. Tip into a bowl, add the breadcrumbs and oil and season well. Mix together until combined, then set aside.

Preheat the oven to 180°C (350°F), Gas Mark 4. Carefully transfer the vegetables to an ovenproof dish. Sprinkle the walnut breadcrumbs and grated cheese evenly over the top, then transfer to the oven and cook for 30 minutes until golden brown and the cheese is melted and bubbling. Leave to stand for 5–10 minutes. Serve with steamed greens, or with a nut roast or whole baked cauliflower.

This summer pie is a twist on the classic Greek spanakopita. It is a brilliant way of using up all your greens – you can also use spinach or spring greens. The vegetables are cooked in the slow cooker, then the pie is assembled and baked in the oven.

SERVES 6 • PREPARATION TIME 50 MINUTES • COOKING TIME 2 HOURS

LEMONY GREENS & FETA FILO PIE

500 g (1 lb) Swiss chard, sliced
200 g (7 oz) cavolo nero, stems removed and leaves shredded
3 garlic cloves, finely chopped
grated zest and juice of 1 unwaxed lemon
100 ml (3½ fl oz) vegetable stock
3 eggs, beaten
good grating of nutmeg
250 g (8 oz) feta cheese, crumbled
20 g (¾ oz) parsley, chopped
small handful of mint leaves, chopped
270 g (9 oz) packet filo pastry sheets
100 g (3½ oz) butter, melted
1 tablespoon sesame seeds
salt and pepper

green salad leaves, to serve

Put the chard, cavolo nero, garlic, lemon juice and stock into the slow cooker. Season well with salt and pepper and stir. Cover with the lid and cook on high for 2 hours until the vegetables are tender.

Line a sieve with kitchen paper, then tip the cooked greens into the sieve and drain, using more kitchen paper to squeeze out as much liquid as possible. Transfer to a large bowl and leave to cool, then add the eggs, a good grating of nutmeg, the feta, chopped herbs and lemon zest and mix together. Set aside.

Preheat the oven to 200°C (400°F), Gas Mark 6. Reserve 2 filo sheets for the top of the pie. Brush 1 of the remaining sheets of filo pastry with melted butter, then place in a 20 cm (8 inch) springform or round cake tin to cover half the bottom of the tin and up the sides, leaving a generous amount of overhanging pastry. Repeat with more layers of buttered filo, working your way around the tin until the bottom and sides are covered.

Tip the chard mixture into the filo case and smooth the surface, then fold the overhanging sheets of filo over the top to enclose the filling. Brush the reserved filo sheets with butter, then scrunch up and place on top. Sprinkle with the sesame seeds. Place the tin on a baking sheet and bake in the middle of the oven for 30 minutes until crisp and golden brown.

Leave to cool in the tin for about 10 minutes, then carefully remove the pie from the tin and slide on to a plate. Serve with a fresh green salad. It's great with buttery new potatoes too.

These stuffed peppers are so easy to prepare and make a fantastic starter or main meal for entertaining guests. The spelt and halloumi stuffing is delicious – however, you can easily replace these with cooked pearl barley, couscous or rice, and feta.

SERVES 4 • PREPARATION TIME 35 MINUTES • COOKING TIME 2 HOURS

SPELT & HALLOUMI STUFFED PEPPERS

150 g (5 oz) pearled spelt, rinsed

4 large peppers

100 g (3½ oz) halloumi cheese, finely chopped

100 g (3½ oz) cherry tomatoes, finely chopped

3 spring onions, finely chopped

small handful of mixed fresh herbs, such as parsley, mint, coriander or dill, chopped

1 tablespoon olive oil, plus extra for greasing and drizzling

1 tablespoon tomato purée

salt and pepper

Put the spelt into a saucepan, cover with cold water and bring to the boil, then reduce the heat and simmer for about 20 minutes, or according to the packet instructions, until tender. Drain and leave to cool slightly.

Meanwhile, prepare the peppers. Using a knife, level off the bottom of each pepper so it stands flat, making sure not to cut through the flesh. Cut off the tops so each has a lid, then scoop out the core and all the seeds.

Mix together the cooked spelt and remaining ingredients in a bowl, then season with salt and pepper. Grease the bottom of the slow cooker pot with some oil.

Stuff each pepper with the spelt mixture, pressing it down so the peppers are well filled, then top each with a lid. Place in the slow cooker so the peppers stand upright, then drizzle each with a little oil. Cover with the lid and cook on high for 2 hours until cooked through and tender.

Serve warm with herbed potatoes and sautéed green vegetables. Alternatively, leave to cool and serve cold with a fresh green salad.

This hearty bean and vegetable stew, packed full of flavour, uses vegetarian sausages for a twist on a French cassoulet.

SERVES 4 • PREPARATION TIME 35 MINUTES • COOKING TIME 3 HOURS

VEGETARIAN SAUSAGE & WHITE BEAN STEW

3 tablespoons olive oil

1 onion, chopped

2 garlic cloves, sliced

8 vegetarian sausages

2 carrots, thickly sliced

1 leek, trimmed, cleaned and thickly sliced

400 g (13 oz) can chopped tomatoes

200 ml (7 fl oz) red wine

2 tablespoons tomato purée

2 roasted red peppers from a jar, thinly sliced

pinch of dried chilli flakes

½ teaspoon dried oregano

2 rosemary sprigs

2 thyme sprigs

400 g (13 oz) can haricot or cannellini beans, drained and rinsed

100 g (3½ oz) kale, stems removed and leaves roughly torn

salt and pepper

2 tablespoons chopped parsley, to garnish

mashed potato, to serve

Heat 2 tablespoons of the oil in a large frying pan, add the onion and fry over a medium-low heat for 5 minutes until soft and translucent, then stir in the garlic and fry for 3 minutes until the onion and garlic are lightly golden. Transfer to the slow cooker.

Return the pan to the heat, add the remaining oil and the vegetarian sausages and fry for about 15 minutes until golden brown on all sides.

Transfer the sausages to the slow cooker and add the carrots, leek, chopped tomatoes, wine, tomato purée, red peppers, chilli flakes and oregano. Fill up the chopped tomatoes can with water, right to the top, then pour in. Season well with salt and pepper, then add the rosemary and thyme. Cover with the lid and cook on high for 2 hours.

Stir in the beans, replace the lid and cook for a further 50 minutes, then add the kale. Replace the lid and continue to cook for 10 minutes until the kale is tender. Adjust the seasoning to taste.

Garnish with the chopped parsley and serve with creamy mashed potato.

These stuffed cabbage leaves are a version of the Polish favourite, golumpki. Typically stuffed with minced pork or beef, this vegetarian version uses wild rice, chestnuts and cranberries.

SERVES 4 • PREPARATION TIME 20 MINUTES • COOKING TIME 2 HOURS

STUFFED CABBAGE LEAVES

1 tablespoon olive oil

1 onion, finely sliced

250 g (8 oz) pouch of pre-cooked mixed rice, such as basmati and wild rice

150 g (5 oz) cooked chestnuts, chopped

75 g (3 oz) dried cranberries

50 g (2 oz) sauerkraut

1 tablespoon chopped dill

1 tablespoon chopped chives, plus extra to garnish

8 large Savoy cabbage leaves

300 ml (½ pint) vegetable stock

1 tablespoon apple cider vinegar

1 tablespoon honey

salt and pepper

soured cream, to serve

Heat the oil in a frying pan, add the onion and fry over a medium-low heat for 5 minutes until soft and translucent, then stir in the rice and chestnuts and cook for a few minutes until heated through. Tip into a bowl and add the dried cranberries, sauerkraut and chopped herbs. Season well with salt and pepper and mix together.

Spoon about 2 tablespoons of the rice mixture into each cabbage leaf, then wrap over the leaves to enclose the filling. Arrange in the slow cooker pot, seam sides downwards to keep them intact.

Mix together the stock, vinegar and honey in a jug, then pour over the stuffed leaves. Cover with the lid and cook on high for 2 hours until the cabbage is tender.

Garnish with extra chopped chives and serve with soured cream.

This biryani takes a little time, but the results are worth it.

SERVES 4 • PREPARATION TIME 55 MINUTES, PLUS SOAKING • COOKING TIME 2 HOURS

VEGETABLE BIRYANI

250 g (8 oz) basmati rice

50 g (2 oz) cashew nuts

3 tablespoons coconut oil, plus extra for greasing

3 red onions, finely sliced

2 green chillies (deseeded if liked), finely chopped

2 carrots, chopped

2 potatoes, peeled and cubed

½ cauliflower, cut into small florets

1 teaspoon garam masala

1 teaspoon ground cumin

½ teaspoon ground cinnamon

5 garlic cloves, crushed

100 g (3½ oz) frozen peas

2 tablespoons tomato purée

100 g (3½ oz) passata (sieved tomatoes)

4 cardamom pods

3 cloves

1 teaspoon salt

2 tablespoons milk

pinch of saffron threads

1 tablespoon raisins

small handful of coriander, chopped, to garnish

Put the rice into a bowl, cover with cold water and leave to soak for 30 minutes. Meanwhile, heat a large, dry frying pan over a medium-low heat, add the cashews and toast for about 5 minutes, stirring frequently, until golden brown. Remove from the pan and leave to cool slightly, then roughly chop. Set aside.

Heat 1 tablespoon of the coconut oil in the frying pan, add the onions and fry over a medium-high heat for about 10 minutes until golden brown and caramelized. Remove with a slotted spoon and set aside.

Heat another tablespoon of the coconut oil in the frying pan, add the chillies and fry over a medium heat for 2 minutes. Add the carrots, potatoes and cauliflower and cook for 5 minutes until they begin to turn golden brown. Add the garam masala, cumin, cinnamon and garlic. Cook for a few minutes, mixing well. Stir in the peas, tomato purée and passata and heat through for 2 minutes. Set aside.

Drain the rice. Bring a large saucepan of water to the boil, add the rice, cardamom, cloves and salt and cook for about 7 minutes until nearly cooked. Drain, tip into a bowl and stir through the remaining coconut oil. Set aside.

Heat the milk in a separate saucepan until warm. Remove from the heat, stir in the saffron and leave to infuse for 10 minutes.

Grease the slow cooker pot with coconut oil. Add half the vegetables and spread in an even layer, then add half the rice and spread evenly. Scatter over half the fried onions, half the raisins and half the toasted cashews. Repeat. Pour the saffron milk evenly over the surface.

Cover with the lid and cook on high for 2 hours until the rice and vegetables are tender. Sprinkle with the coriander and serve.

This dhal is fragrant and comforting. You can serve it with rice to make it more substantial, but the lentils are filling enough.

SERVES 4 • PREPARATION TIME 20 MINUTES • COOKING TIME 2 HOURS

COCONUT DHAL WITH PANEER

1 tablespoon coconut oil

1 onion, chopped

3 garlic cloves, finely chopped

1 thumb-sized piece of fresh root ginger, peeled and finely chopped

1 red chilli, deseeded and finely chopped

1 teaspoon ground cumin

1 teaspoon mustard seeds

2 teaspoons turmeric

1 teaspoon curry powder

350 g (11½ oz) red lentils

400 ml (14 fl oz) can coconut milk

600 ml (1 pint) vegetable stock

150 g (5 oz) fresh spinach leaves

small handful of coriander, chopped

salt and pepper

FOR THE TOPPINGS

1 tablespoon groundnut oil, plus extra if necessary

200 g (7 oz) paneer, cut into bite-sized cubes

10 curry leaves

1 tablespoon mustard seeds

TO SERVE

warm roti breads

mango chutney

Heat the coconut oil in a large frying pan, add the onion and fry over a medium-low heat for 5 minutes until soft and translucent, then stir in the garlic, ginger, chilli and dried spices and fry for a few minutes until fragrant.

Transfer the onion mixture to the slow cooker, add the lentils, coconut milk and stock and season with salt and pepper, then stir well until combined. Cook on high for 2 hours until the lentils are tender and soft, and the sauce thick and creamy.

Turn off the slow cooker, then stir in the spinach and coriander. Replace the lid and leave to wilt in the residual heat.

Meanwhile, heat the groundnut oil in a frying pan, add the paneer cubes and cook over a medium-high heat for about 1 minute on each side until golden brown, carefully turning the pieces to ensure they are golden on all sides. Remove from the pan with a slotted spoon and drain on kitchen paper.

Add a little more groundnut oil to the pan, if needed, then add the curry leaves and mustard seeds and fry for 1–2 minutes until the seeds begin to pop.

Spoon the dhal into serving bowls, then top with the crispy paneer cubes and a drizzle of the spice-infused oil, with the curry leaves and mustard seeds. Serve with warm roti breads and mango chutney, and dollops of yogurt, if liked.

Sweet potato is perfect in curries as it helps thicken the sauce as it cooks. You can add other vegetables to this curry if you like – cauliflower or butternut squash work well. If you choose green vegetables, such as green beans, spinach or mangetout, add these nearer the end of the cooking time.

SERVES 4 • PREPARATION TIME 10 MINUTES • COOKING TIME 3 HOURS

SWEET POTATO CURRY WITH TOASTED CASHEWS

200 g (7 oz) red lentils, rinsed

1 onion, chopped

2 garlic cloves, crushed

1 thumb-sized piece of fresh root ginger, peeled and grated

3 sweet potatoes, peeled and cubed

2 tablespoons red Thai curry paste

1 teaspoon garam masala

1 teaspoon turmeric

2 kaffir lime leaves

2 tablespoons tomato purée

500 ml (17 fl oz) vegetable stock

400 ml (14 fl oz) can coconut milk

100 g (3½ oz) cashew nuts

salt and pepper

TO SERVE

1 red chilli, deseeded and finely sliced

handful of coriander, chopped

cooked brown or wild rice

Put all the ingredients except the cashews into the slow cooker and stir together until the tomato purée is incorporated and the sauce well combined. Cover with the lid and cook on high for 3 hours until the lentils and sweet potatoes are tender and the sauce is thick.

When almost ready to serve, heat a large, dry frying pan over a medium-low heat, add the cashews and toast for about 5 minutes, stirring frequently, until golden brown. Alternatively, put on a baking tray and roast in an oven preheated to 180°C (350°F), Gas Mark 4, for 2 minutes. Remove the tray from the oven and carefully shake to mix the cashews. Return to the oven for about 3 minutes until the cashews are golden brown. Leave to cool slightly, then roughly chop.

Season the curry to taste with salt and pepper, then spoon into serving bowls and sprinkle with the toasted cashews, sliced chilli and chopped coriander. Serve with brown or wild rice.

Sag aloo paneer is an Indian dish, which simply translates as spinach potato paneer. The slow-cooked spinach and spices are full of flavour.

SERVES 4 • PREPARATION TIME 25 MINUTES • COOKING TIME 2 HOURS 20 MINUTES

SAG ALOO PANEER

1 tablespoon coconut oil

1 onion, chopped

4 garlic cloves, chopped

5 cm (2 inch) piece of fresh root ginger, peeled and chopped

1 tablespoon garam masala

1 tablespoon turmeric

1 tablespoon ground cumin

1 tablespoon ground coriander

1 teaspoon mustard seeds

1 green chilli, deseeded and finely chopped

875 g (1¾ lb) frozen spinach, defrosted, drained and chopped

100 g (3½ oz) baby new potatoes, peeled and chopped into bite-sized cubes

200 g (7 oz) passata (sieved tomatoes)

400 ml (14 fl oz) can coconut milk

200 g (7 oz) fresh spinach leaves, finely chopped

200 g (7 oz) paneer, cut into bite-sized cubes

salt

steamed basmati rice, to serve

Heat the coconut oil in a frying pan, add the onion and fry over a medium-low heat for 5 minutes until soft and translucent, then stir in the garlic, ginger, dried spices and green chilli and fry for a few minutes until fragrant.

Transfer the onion mixture to the slow cooker, add the defrosted spinach, potatoes, passata and coconut milk and season well with salt. Mix together, then cover with the lid and cook on high for 2 hours.

Stir in the fresh spinach and paneer cubes, replace the lid and cook, still on high, for a further 20 minutes until the sauce has reduced and thickened.

Serve with steamed basmati rice, or warm roti breads if you prefer, or as a side dish with other curries.

Jackfruit is a brilliant alternative to meat and in this recipe you can barely taste the difference. Cooked in hoisin sauce and served with crisp cucumber and spring onions wrapped up in pancakes, it is a fantastic vegetarian version of the crispy duck takeaway favourite.

SERVES 4 • PREPARATION TIME 15 MINUTES • COOKING TIME 2 HOURS

CHINESE HOISIN PULLED JACKFRUIT

1 tablespoon sesame oil

2 garlic cloves, crushed

3 cm (1¼ inch) piece of fresh root ginger, peeled and grated

2 x 400 g (13 oz) cans jackfruit, drained

1 teaspoon Chinese five spice

2 tablespoons soy sauce

3 tablespoons hoisin sauce, plus extra for brushing and serving

1 teaspoon mirin

TO SERVE

8 Chinese pancakes

½ cucumber, cut into long, thin strips

handful of spring onions, cut into long, thin strips

black and white sesame seeds

Heat the sesame oil in a frying pan, and add the garlic and ginger. Fry over a medium-low heat for a few minutes until softened and fragrant.

Transfer the mixture to the slow cooker, add the jackfruit, five spice, soy sauce, hoisin sauce and mirin and mix together. Cover with the lid and cook on high for 2 hours.

Preheat the grill. Carefully remove the jackfruit from the slow cooker and spread out on a baking tray. Brush with more hoisin sauce, then place under the grill for 5 minutes until caramelized and browned on the edges.

Serve with Chinese pancakes, strips of cucumber and spring onions, some extra hoisin sauce and a sprinkle of sesame seeds.

MAINS: MORE THAN 3½ HOURS

Another French classic, this time an onion soup. The best versions are cooked for a long time over a low heat, so the onions become very soft and the broth is full of flavour. This recipe is worth the long cook time – you will never rush a French onion soup again!

SERVES 4 • PREPARATION TIME 20 MINUTES • COOKING TIME 12 HOURS

FRENCH ONION SOUP WITH MUSTARDY EMMENTAL CROUTONS

100 g (3½ oz) butter
2 tablespoons olive oil
875 g (1¾ lb) white onions, sliced
1 teaspoon sea salt
1.5 litres (2½ pints) vegetable stock
150 ml (¼ pint) white wine
2 tablespoons balsamic vinegar
3 thyme sprigs
pepper
chopped thyme, to garnish

FOR THE CROUTONS
1 baguette, cut into 8 x 1 cm (½ inch) slices
olive oil, for drizzling
25 g (1 oz) Dijon mustard
100 g (3½ oz) Emmental cheese, grated

Put the butter and oil into the slow cooker, turn on to low and leave until the butter begins to melt, then add the onions and salt and mix together until the onions are well coated. Cover with the lid and cook for 4 hours until the onions are soft, tender and caramelized, stirring occasionally to ensure the onions are not sticking to the pot.

Pour in the stock, wine, balsamic vinegar and thyme, replace the lid and cook, still on low, for a further 6 hours until the soup is reduced and full of flavour. Season to taste with salt and pepper.

When ready to serve, preheat the grill. Drizzle the baguette slices with a little oil, then cook under the grill until lightly toasted on each side. Spread each slice with a thin layer of the mustard.

Ladle the soup into 4 heatproof bowls, then top each one with 2 slices of the toasted baguette and sprinkle liberally with the grated cheese. Place the bowls under the grill and cook for 3–5 minutes until the cheese has melted and is bubbly and golden.

Serve immediately, sprinkled with chopped thyme.

1 tablespoon olive oil, plus extra
    to serve
1 onion, chopped
2 large carrots, chopped
2 celery sticks, chopped
2 rosemary sprigs
1 bay leaf
1 teaspoon dried oregano
400 g (13 oz) can chopped
    tomatoes
1 tablespoon tomato purée
1.5 litres (2½ pints) vegetable
    stock
400 g (13 oz) can borlotti beans,
    drained and rinsed
100 g (3½ oz) ditalini or other
    small dried pasta shapes
1 courgette, chopped
handful of fresh spinach leaves
salt and pepper

TARRAGON PESTO
50 g (2 oz) blanched hazelnuts
1 bunch of tarragon
½ bunch of parsley
100 ml (3½ fl oz) olive oil
juice of ½ lemon
1 small garlic clove, crushed
50 g (2 oz) vegetarian Italian
    hard cheese, grated, plus
    extra to serve

A minestrone is a hearty soup originating from Italy, packed full of vegetables, beans and pasta. This version uses borlotti beans, which have a beautiful flavour, and a small variety of pasta shape called ditalini, which is perfect for soup. It is served topped with a delicious tarragon pesto, which lifts the soup and makes it sing.

**SERVES 4 • PREPARATION TIME 25 MINUTES
COOKING TIME 3 HOURS 40 MINUTES**

MINESTRONE SOUP

Heat the olive oil in a large frying pan, add the onion, carrots and celery and fry over a medium-low heat for about 8 minutes until beginning to soften.

Transfer the vegetables to the slow cooker, add the herbs, chopped tomatoes, tomato purée and stock and mix together well, then season with salt and pepper. Cover with the lid and cook on high for 3 hours 10 minutes.

Meanwhile, make the tarragon pesto. Heat a large, dry frying pan over a medium-low heat, add the hazelnuts and toast for about 5 minutes, stirring frequently, until golden brown. Remove from the pan and leave to cool. Put the toasted hazelnuts into a food processor, add the remaining ingredients and process until fairly smooth (a few chunky bits are quite nice). Season to taste and set aside.

Stir the borlotti beans and dried pasta into the soup, replace the lid and cook, still on high, for a further 20 minutes, then add the courgette and continue to cook for 10 minutes until the pasta and courgette are tender. Stir through the spinach so it wilts, then adjust the seasoning to taste.

Ladle the soup into bowls and top each one with 1 teaspoon of the pesto, a drizzle of olive oil and some extra grated cheese.

Conchiglie is a type of pasta that translates as 'sea shell' in Italian due to its shape. The large variety are perfect for stuffing in this comforting, one-pot pasta dish.

SERVES 4 • PREPARATION TIME 25 MINUTES • COOKING TIME 4 HOURS

GOATS' CHEESE, LEEK & SPINACH CONCHIGLIE BAKE

1 tablespoon olive oil, plus extra for greasing

2 leeks, trimmed and cleaned, 1 chopped and 1 sliced into rounds

875 g (1¾ lb) passata (sieved tomatoes)

50 g (2 oz) ready-made vegetarian basil pesto

150 g (5 oz) soft goats' cheese

150 g (5 oz) ricotta cheese

100 g (3½ oz) frozen spinach, defrosted and drained

300 g (10 oz) dried large conchiglie pasta shells

100 g (3½ oz) mozzarella cheese, torn

salt and pepper

basil leaves, torn, to garnish

Heat the oil in a frying pan, add the chopped leek and fry over a medium-low heat for 4–5 minutes until softened, then leave to cool.

Mix together the passata, pesto and some salt and pepper in a large bowl. Set aside.

Put the cooled leeks, goats' cheese, ricotta and spinach into a separate bowl and mix together, then season well. Carefully spoon the cheese mixture into the pasta shells.

Grease the slow cooker pot with oil. Spoon in half the passata mixture in an even layer, then add the filled pasta shells, open edge upwards, in an even layer and dot the leek slices around them. Spoon over the remaining passata and top with the mozzarella. Cover with the lid and cook on low for 4 hours until the sauce has thickened and the pasta is tender.

Serve sprinkled with torn basil leaves.

This meat-free Bolognese recipe is slow-cooked and packed full of flavour. The use of mushrooms and walnuts adds a 'meaty' flavour to the dish, making it similar to the original.

SERVES 6 • PREPARATION TIME 25 MINUTES • COOKING TIME 4 HOURS

MUSHROOM BOLOGNESE

2 tablespoons olive oil

1 onion, finely chopped

2 carrots, finely chopped

1 celery stick, finely chopped

3 garlic cloves, crushed

1 teaspoon fennel seeds

450 g (14½ oz) chestnut mushrooms, finely chopped

125 g (4 oz) walnuts

2 tablespoons tomato purée

1 teaspoon dried oregano

200 ml (7 fl oz) red wine

2 x 400 g (13 oz) cans chopped tomatoes

500 ml (17 fl oz) vegetable or mushroom stock

1 teaspoon soy sauce

1 bay leaf

salt and pepper

TO SERVE

cooked tagliatelle

basil leaves

grated vegetarian Italian hard cheese

Heat the oil in a large frying pan, add the onion, carrots and celery and cook over a medium heat for about 8 minutes until softened. Stir in the garlic, fennel seeds and mushrooms and cook for about 5 minutes until the mushrooms are golden brown and the liquid released from the mushrooms has evaporated.

Meanwhile, place the walnuts in a food processor and process until finely chopped. Alternatively, finely chop with a sharp knife.

Transfer the mushroom mixture to the slow cooker, add the chopped walnuts and all the remaining ingredients and mix together. Cover with the lid and cook on high for 4 hours until the sauce has reduced and thickened. Season well with salt and pepper and remove the bay leaf.

Serve hot with cooked tagliatelle, or spaghetti or Creamy Cheesy Polenta (see page 39) if you prefer, sprinkled with a few basil leaves and a grating of cheese. Alternatively, leave the sauce to cool, then freeze for up to 6 months.

This tomato sauce is a brilliant staple – you can easily double up the recipe to make big batches of it, then freeze for whenever it is needed. It is very versatile and can be used as a base for so many dishes: pasta sauces, pizza toppings and stews.

MAKES 1 LITRE (1¾ PINTS) • PREPARATION TIME 15 MINUTES • COOKING TIME 8 HOURS

ULTIMATE SLOW-COOKED TOMATO SAUCE

2 tablespoons olive oil

1 onion, chopped

4 garlic cloves, crushed

3 x 400 g (13 oz) cans chopped tomatoes (best quality possible)

2 tablespoons tomato purée

200 ml (7 fl oz) red wine

200 ml (7 fl oz) vegetable stock

1 teaspoon dried oregano

½ teaspoon dried basil

1 bay leaf

1 teaspoon caster sugar

salt and pepper

Heat the oil in a frying pan, add the onion and fry over a medium-low heat for 5 minutes until soft and translucent, then stir in the garlic and fry for 3 minutes until the onion and garlic are lightly golden.

Transfer the onion mixture to the slow cooker, add the remaining ingredients and mix well. Cover with the lid and cook on low for 8 hours until the sauce is thick and full of flavour.

Remove the bay leaf. If you prefer a smoother sauce, leave to cool slightly, then purée until smooth while still in the slow cooker pot using a stick blender.

Leave to cool, then store in the refrigerator for up to 5 days or freeze for up to 6 months.

The base of this dish is a flavoursome and slow-cooked ratatouille, which can be served simply on its own or with pasta. However, for a more unique dish, this bake is topped with a crunchy ciabatta crust, which works perfectly to soak up all the tomatoey juices.

SERVES 4 • PREPARATION TIME 45 MINUTES • COOKING TIME 6 HOURS

RATATOUILLE BAKE WITH CIABATTA CRUST

1 tablespoon olive oil

1 red onion, sliced

3 garlic cloves, chopped

2 aubergines, chopped

2 red peppers, cored, deseeded and chopped

1 yellow pepper, cored, deseeded and chopped

1 green courgette, chopped

1 yellow courgette, chopped

2 tablespoons tomato purée

400 g (13 oz) can chopped tomatoes

1 tablespoon balsamic vinegar

1 bay leaf

1 rosemary sprig

1 teaspoon caster sugar

salt and pepper

FOR THE TOPPING

200 g (7 oz) ciabatta bread, torn into pieces

2 tablespoons olive oil

1 teaspoon dried oregano

Heat the oil in a large frying pan, add the onion and fry over a medium heat for a few minutes until softened. Stir in the garlic, aubergines and peppers and fry for a few minutes, then add the courgettes and cook for a further few minutes until all the vegetables have softened.

Transfer the vegetables to the slow cooker, add the remaining ingredients and mix together until well combined. Season with salt and pepper. Cover with the lid and cook on low for 6 hours until the sauce is thickened and the vegetables are tender.

Preheat the oven to 180°C (350°F), Gas Mark 4. Mix together all the topping ingredients in a small bowl, then season. Carefully spoon the ratatouille into a baking dish, then top with the ciabatta mixture. Bake for 15–20 minutes until the topping is golden and crunchy. Leave to stand for 5 minutes before serving.

This recipe makes one large loaf and, although it is best served fresh, it can easily be sliced and frozen for later.

MAKES 1 LARGE LOAF • PREPARATION TIME 25 MINUTES, PLUS STANDING COOKING TIME 3 HOURS

SEEDED MALT BREAD

1 tablespoon olive oil, plus extra
   for greasing
200 ml (7 fl oz) lukewarm water
1 teaspoon sugar
1 teaspoon fast-action dried
   yeast
1 teaspoon salt
400 g (13 oz) malted bread
   flour, plus extra for dusting
60 g (2¼ oz) mixed seeds,
   such as sunflower, pumpkin,
   linseeds, poppy or sesame

salted butter, to serve

Grease a 900 g (2 lb) loaf tin with oil and set aside. Put the measured water and sugar into a large bowl and stir together until slightly dissolved. Sprinkle the yeast over the surface and whisk in, then leave to stand for 10 minutes until the surface is bubbly and frothy.

Whisk in the salt and oil, then add the flour and mix until well combined. Tip the dough out on to a lightly floured surface and knead for about 10 minutes until soft and supple.

Transfer the dough to a bowl, then place the bowl in the slow cooker. Cover with a clean tea towel, then cover with the lid. Turn the slow cooker setting to warm and leave the dough to rise for 30 minutes until doubled in size. Alternatively, if your slow cooker does not have a warm setting, place the dough in a bowl, cover with the tea towel and leave in a warm place to rise.

Remove the dough and place on a lightly floured surface. Knock back the dough, then knead in the seeds until well distributed. Transfer to the loaf tin, shaping it to fit into the corners. Place in the slow cooker, still on warm, or in a warm place, re-cover with the tea towel and leave to rise for a further 30 minutes until doubled in size again.

Carefully slash the top of the bread with a serrated knife. Re-cover with the tea towel, cover with the lid and cook on high for 2 hours until the bread is well risen and has a hard crust. Carefully remove the tin from the slow cooker using oven gloves. Transfer the loaf to a wire rack to cool. Serve warm or toasted, with salted butter, or leave to cool completely, then cut into slices and freeze for up to 5 months.

Slow-cooked red cabbage is an essential part of many people's Christmas day meals. This recipe is full of flavour and making it in your slow cooker allows you space in the oven for other dishes.

SERVES 6 • PREPARATION TIME 10 MINUTES • COOKING TIME 5 HOURS

BRAISED RED CABBAGE WITH CIDER

500 g (1 lb) red cabbage, shredded

2 red onions, sliced

2 Granny Smith apples, peeled, cored and chopped

150 ml (¼ pint) cider

2 tablespoons soft brown sugar

1 tablespoon balsamic vinegar

1 cinnamon stick or ½ teaspoon ground cinnamon

Put the cabbage, onions and apples into the slow cooker and mix well. Stir together the cider, sugar and vinegar in a jug, then pour over the vegetables. Add the cinnamon.

Cover with the lid. Cook on low for 5 hours until the cabbage is soft and tender. Remove the cinnamon stick, if using, before serving.

Braising globe artichokes in this way is a favourite for many in France. Simply served with a Dijon mustard dressing they make an elegant starter for a dinner party.

SERVES 4 AS A STARTER • PREPARATION TIME 10 MINUTES • COOKING TIME 4 HOURS

BRAISED ARTICHOKES WITH MUSTARD VINAIGRETTE

4 globe artichokes
4 garlic cloves, crushed
2 tablespoons olive oil
100 ml (3½ fl oz) vegetable stock
salt and pepper

MUSTARD VINAIGRETTE
5 tablespoons olive oil
3 tablespoons white wine vinegar
2 teaspoons Dijon mustard
salt and pepper

Prepare the artichokes by cutting off the base stalks and trimming the stems so that the artichokes will sit flat in the slow cooker. Trim the tops of the leaves to remove the sharp ends. Rinse the artichokes under cold water to wash away any dirt between the leaves. Press the leaves so they splay out slightly.

Mix the crushed garlic, olive oil and some salt and pepper in a small bowl. Rub the mixture all over the artichokes and in between the leaves.

Put the artichokes into the slow cooker, then pour the stock around them. Cover with the lid and cook on low for 4 hours until the artichokes are tender when a knife is inserted.

When almost ready to serve, make the vinaigrette. Whisk together all the ingredients in a serving bowl.

Serve the warm artichokes with the vinaigrette alongside to dip the leaves into.

These stuffed mushrooms are so simple to make but are a great starter for guests at your dinner party – they look and taste like you have made more effort than you have!

SERVES 4 AS A STARTER • PREPARATION TIME 10 MINUTES • COOKING TIME 4 HOURS

SUN-DRIED TOMATO & OLIVE-STUFFED MUSHROOMS

4 portobello mushrooms

2 garlic cloves, crushed

1 tablespoon ready-made vegetarian basil pesto

50 g (2 oz) mascarpone cheese

4 sun-dried tomatoes, finely chopped

8 pitted black olives, finely chopped

20 g (¾ oz) vegetarian Italian hard cheese, grated

1 tablespoon chopped parsley, to garnish

mixed salad leaves, to serve

Brush the mushrooms clean and remove the stalks. Place each mushroom, gill side up, on a square of foil large enough to allow the edges of the foil to fold upwards over the mushrooms to create 'tent' parcels.

Mix together the garlic, pesto, mascarpone, tomatoes and olives in a small bowl. Spoon equal amounts of the mixture into each mushroom and smooth the tops. Sprinkle over the grated cheese.

Fold up and seal the foil over each mushroom, then place the parcels in the slow cooker. Cover with the lid and cook on low for 4 hours until the mushrooms are tender but still holding their shape.

Carefully remove the parcels from the slow cooker, then the mushrooms from the foil and garnish with the chopped parsley. Serve with a mixed salad – these are particularly good with a rocket or watercress salad.

A slow cooker acts as the perfect environment to confit tomatoes and garlic for this delicious tart. The confit mixture can be stored in the refrigerator and is delicious served in salads or sandwiches.

SERVES 6–8 • PREPARATION TIME 45 MINUTES, PLUS COOLING COOKING TIME 4 HOURS

CONFIT TOMATO TART

500 g (1 lb) block shortcrust pastry
flour, for dusting
2 tablespoons olive oil
3 large onions, thinly sliced
1 tablespoon balsamic vinegar
2 tablespoons soft brown sugar
100 g (3½ oz) goats' cheese log with rind on, cut into thin slices
salt and pepper
thyme leaves, to garnish

CONFIT TOMATOES
1 kg (2 lb) mixed-colour cherry tomatoes
10 garlic cloves, peeled
a few rosemary and thyme sprigs
2 teaspoons sea salt
375 ml (13 fl oz) olive oil

Put the cherry tomatoes, garlic, herbs, salt and oil into the slow cooker and mix together well. Cover with the lid and cook on low for 4 hours until the tomatoes are soft, tender and wrinkled. Carefully remove the slow cooker pot from the cooker using oven gloves and leave to cool (the confit mixture can be stored in an airtight container or sterilized jar in the refrigerator for up to 2 weeks).

Roll out the pastry on a lightly floured work surface, then use to line a 20 cm (8 inch) fluted tart tin. Chill in the refrigerator for 10 minutes. Preheat the oven to 180°C (350°F), Gas Mark 4. Line the case with baking paper, fill with baking beans and bake in the oven for 10 minutes. Remove from the oven and carefully lift out the paper and beans, then return to the oven and bake for a further 5 minutes until lightly golden and chalky to the touch. Leave to cool.

Meanwhile, heat the oil in a large frying pan, add the onions and a pinch of salt and fry over a low heat for about 15 minutes until very soft and golden brown. Stir in the vinegar and sugar and cook for a further 5 minutes until the onions are caramelized and all the liquid has been absorbed. Leave to cool slightly.

Increase the oven temperature to 200°C (400°F), Gas Mark 6. Spread a layer of the caramelized onions over the base of the baked pastry case. Using a slotted spoon, add a layer of the confit tomatoes, ensuring not to add too much oil. Top with the goats' cheese, drizzle with a little of the confit oil and season with pepper. Bake for 10 minutes until warmed through. Serve sprinkled with thyme leaves.

This comforting, autumnal pie is brilliant for feeding the family. Mix and match the root vegetables with what you have: white potatoes, celeriac and turnip all work well.

SERVES 4 • PREPARATION TIME 30 MINUTES • COOKING TIME 6 HOURS 10 MINUTES

ROOT VEGETABLE PUFF PASTRY PIE

1 red onion, chopped

2 carrots, chopped

2 parsnips, chopped

1 sweet potato, peeled and chopped

2 floury potatoes (such as Maris Piper), peeled and chopped

3 garlic cloves, crushed

1 tablespoon thyme leaves

2 tablespoons plain flour

750 ml (1¼ pints) vegetable stock

75 ml (3 fl oz) double cream

100 g (3½ oz) frozen peas

1 tablespoon wholegrain mustard

1 egg, beaten

1 sheet puff pastry

salt and pepper

steamed greens, to serve

Put the chopped vegetables, garlic and thyme into the slow cooker, then sprinkle over the flour and season well with salt and pepper. Toss the vegetables until well coated in the flour. Pour in the stock and stir together until well combined and there are no lumps of flour. Cover with the lid and cook on low for 6 hours.

Stir in the cream, frozen peas and mustard, replace the lid and cook, still on low, for a further 10 minutes until the sauce is thickened and creamy and the vegetables are tender.

Preheat the oven to 200°C (400°F), Gas Mark 6. Carefully spoon the vegetable mixture into a 23 x 33 cm (9 x 13 inch) ovenproof dish. Brush a little of the beaten egg around the top edges of the dish, then drape over the pastry sheet, pressing the edges to seal. Trim off any excess pastry, then brush the top with the remaining beaten egg.

Bake in the oven for 10 minutes until the top is golden brown and puffed up. Serve with steamed greens.

This vegetarian stroganoff is full of beautiful wild mushrooms, which give the dish depth and a real 'meaty' and earthy flavour.

SERVES 4 • PREPARATION TIME 35 MINUTES, PLUS SOAKING • COOKING TIME 4 HOURS

CREAMY WILD MUSHROOM STROGANOFF

15 g (½ oz) dried porcini
   mushrooms
400 ml (14 fl oz) boiling water
50 g (2 oz) unsalted butter
400 g (13 oz) shallots, sliced
3 garlic cloves, sliced
2 tablespoons thyme leaves
400 g (13 oz) portobello
   mushrooms, sliced
300 g (10 oz) shiitake
   mushrooms, halved
200 g (7 oz) oyster mushrooms,
   sliced lengthways
100 ml (3½ fl oz) white wine
1 tablespoon wholegrain mustard
1 teaspoon vegetarian
   Worcestershire sauce
150 ml (¼ pint) soured cream
small handful of parsley,
   chopped, plus extra to garnish
salt and pepper

Put the porcini mushrooms into a small heatproof bowl and pour over the measured water. Leave to soak until rehydrated.

Meanwhile, heat the butter in a large frying pan, add the shallots and cook over a low heat for about 8 minutes until very soft and translucent. Stir in the garlic and thyme and fry for a few minutes until softened. Add the portobello, shiitake and oyster mushrooms and cook over a medium heat for a further 5 minutes until beginning to soften and caramelize. Pour in the wine and bring to the boil, then reduce the heat and simmer for 1 minute.

Transfer the mushroom mixture to the slow cooker, add the porcini mushrooms and their soaking water, the mustard and Worcestershire sauce and mix together. Season well with salt and pepper.

Cover with the lid and cook on low for 4 hours until the sauce has thickened. Stir in the soured cream and parsley and adjust the seasoning to taste.

Garnish with a little more chopped parsley and serve with cooked rice or pasta, or spooned over Creamy Cheesy Polenta (see page 39).

This meat-free lasagne, topped with crispy sage leaves, is a real crowd-pleaser and perfect for entertaining guests.

SERVES 4 • PREPARATION TIME 1 HOUR • COOKING TIME 3 HOURS

PUMPKIN, BRIE & SAGE LASAGNE

1 pumpkin or butternut squash, about 1 kg (2 lb), peeled, deseeded and chopped

1 onion, chopped

4 garlic cloves, peeled

2 tablespoons oil, plus extra for greasing

350 g (11½ oz) ricotta cheese

1 egg

200 g (7 oz) frozen spinach, defrosted and drained

100 g (3½ oz) vegetarian Italian hard cheese, grated

a little grated nutmeg

6–8 dried lasagne sheets

100 g (3½ oz) vegetarian Brie, crumbled

salt and pepper

CRISPY SAGE LEAVES

2 tablespoons olive oil

20 g (¾ oz) sage leaves

fresh green salad, to serve

Preheat the oven to 180°C (350°F), Gas Mark 4. Put the pumpkin or squash, onion and garlic on a large baking tray and drizzle with the olive oil. Season well with salt and pepper and mix together until the vegetables are well coated. Roast for 25 minutes until tender. Leave to cool slightly, then transfer to a food processor and process until smooth. Adjust the seasoning to taste, then transfer to a bowl.

Clean the food processor bowl, then add the ricotta, egg, spinach, half the grated Italian hard cheese and a little grated nutmeg. Season well and then process until smooth.

Grease the slow cooker pot with some oil. Arrange a layer of lasagne sheets to cover the bottom of the pot evenly. Spoon in half the pumpkin purée, then add half the ricotta mixture and half the crumbled Brie. Repeat with the remaining lasagne, pumpkin, ricotta and Brie. Sprinkle over the remaining grated cheese.

Cover with the lid and cook on low for 3 hours until the lasagne is cooked through and the cheese melted. Preheat the oven to 200°C (400°F), Gas Mark 6. Carefully remove the slow cooker pot from the cooker using oven gloves and transfer to the oven for 15 minutes until golden brown and bubbling.

Meanwhile, make the crispy sage leaves. Heat the oil in a frying pan until hot, add the sage leaves and fry for 30 seconds until sizzling and crisp, taking care in case the oil spits. Remove with a slotted spoon and leave to drain on kitchen paper.

Remove the lasagne from the oven and top with the sage leaves. Leave to stand for 10 minutes before serving with a fresh green salad.

This 'shepherd's pie' uses lentils as a base instead of minced lamb, is packed full of vegetables and has lots of flavour. The celeriac mash topping is a wonderful alternative to mashed potato and elevates this family favourite.

SERVES 6 • PREPARATION TIME 1¼ HOURS, PLUS SOAKING • COOKING TIME 6 HOURS

LENTIL & CELERIAC 'SHEPHERD'S PIE'

25 g (1 oz) dried porcini
    mushrooms
200 ml (7 fl oz) boiling water
2 tablespoons olive oil
2 onions, finely chopped
2 carrots, finely chopped
2 leeks, trimmed, cleaned and
    finely chopped
5 portobello mushrooms, finely
    chopped
50 g (2 oz) shiitake mushrooms,
    finely chopped
3 garlic cloves, crushed
1 tablespoon tomato purée
400 ml (14 fl oz) red wine
1 bouquet garni, made with 1 bay
    leaf, 2 rosemary sprigs and
    2 thyme sprigs
1 star anise
350 g (11½ oz) dried Puy lentils
1 teaspoon yeast extract
1 teaspoon vegetarian
    Worcestershire sauce
1 litre (1¾ pints) vegetable stock

Put the porcini mushrooms into a small heatproof bowl and pour over the measured water. Leave to soak for 15 minutes until rehydrated.

Meanwhile, heat the oil in a large frying pan, add the onions, carrots and leeks and cook over a medium heat for about 8 minutes until softened and the onion is translucent. Add the chopped mushrooms and cook for 5 minutes until beginning to brown. Stir in the garlic and fry for a further 3 minutes.

Transfer the vegetable mixture to the slow cooker. Strain the porcini mushrooms, reserving the soaking liquid, then finely chop. Add the mushrooms and reserved liquid to the slow cooker, then stir in the remaining ingredients. Cover with the lid and cook on low for 6 hours until the lentils are tender and the sauce thick and reduced, stirring occasionally to ensure the sauce is not sticking.

Make the celeriac mash about 30 minutes before the end of the lentil cooking time. Bring the celeriac and potatoes to the boil in a large saucepan of salted water, then reduce the heat and simmer for about 15 minutes until tender and you can easily insert a knife. Drain, then return to the pan and add the butter, milk and mustard. Mash well with a potato masher or pass through a potato ricer for a very smooth mash, then season to taste with salt and pepper. Set aside.

CELERIAC MASH TOPPING

2 celeriac, peeled and cubed

2 large potatoes, peeled and cubed

75 g (3 oz) butter

2 tablespoons milk

1 teaspoon wholegrain mustard

25 g (1 oz) Cheddar cheese, grated

25 g (1 oz) vegetarian Italian hard cheese, grated

salt and pepper

steamed greens, to serve

Season the cooked lentils to taste, then spoon into an ovenproof baking dish, removing the bouquet garni and star anise. Leave to cool slightly.

Preheat the oven to 190°C (375°F), Gas Mark 5. Spoon the mash over the lentils and smooth level with the back of the spoon. Cover generously with the grated cheeses. Place on a baking sheet and bake in the oven for 30 minutes until golden brown and the cheese is melted.

Leave to stand for 5 minutes before serving with steamed greens. Alternatively, leave the dish to cool completely, then freeze for up to 3 months.

2 tablespoons olive oil

2 red onions, chopped

3 garlic cloves, crushed

1 teaspoon smoked paprika

1 teaspoon ground cumin

1 cinnamon stick

1 teaspoon chipotle paste

2 x 400 g (13 oz) cans chopped tomatoes

grated zest and juice of 1 unwaxed lime

2 x 400 g (13 oz) cans black beans, drained and rinsed

salt and pepper

MANGO SALSA

1 ripe mango, peeled and chopped

1 small red onion, finely chopped

¼ cucumber, finely chopped

2 tablespoons chopped coriander

1 red chilli, deseeded and finely chopped

juice of 1 lime

TO SERVE

8 mini flour tortillas

1 ripe avocado, sliced

1 lime, cut into wedges, plus a little extra lime juice

small handful of coriander, roughly chopped

soured cream

The smoky flavours in this black bean chilli develop over the long slow-cooking times. This recipe is great fun for bigger numbers (simply double the quantities for a crowd), as everyone can get involved and build their own tacos.

**SERVES 4 • PREPARATION TIME 25 MINUTES
COOKING TIME 6 HOURS**

BLACK BEAN CHILLI TACOS

Heat the oil in a large frying pan, add the onions and fry over a medium-low heat for 5 minutes until soft and translucent, then stir in the garlic, paprika, cumin and cinnamon and fry for a few minutes until fragrant. Transfer the mixture to the slow cooker and add the remaining chilli ingredients. Season with salt and pepper and mix together until well combined.

Cover with the lid and cook on low for 6 hours until the sauce has reduced and thickened and the flavours have developed. Remove the cinnamon stick before serving.

Make the salsa about 15 minutes before the end of the chilli cooking time. Mix together all the ingredients in a bowl and set aside.

When ready to serve, warm the tortillas in a preheated oven according to the packet instructions. Halve and stone the avocado, then remove the peel and cut the flesh into slices, squeezing over a little lime juice to stop them turning brown.

Top the warmed tortillas with the chilli, mango salsa, avocado slices, chopped coriander and a drizzle of soured cream. Serve with the lime wedges for squeezing over.

This aubergine stew has Greek influences with its use of preserved lemon, feta cheese and toasted pine nuts. Slow cooking the stew means it is sticky, sweet and full of flavour.

SERVES 4 • PREPARATION TIME 35 MINUTES • COOKING TIME 6 HOURS

GREEK AUBERGINE & TOMATO STEW

4 tablespoons olive oil

1 red onion, sliced

2 celery sticks, sliced

3 garlic cloves, crushed

2 aubergines, cut into 3 cm (1¼ inch) chunks

2 x 400 g (13 oz) can chopped tomatoes

400 g (13 oz) can chickpeas, drained

100 ml (3½ fl oz) red wine

2 tablespoons tomato purée

1 tablespoon red wine vinegar

1 teaspoon sugar

1 preserved lemon, finely sliced

salt and pepper

TO SERVE

1 tablespoon toasted pine nuts

50 g (2 oz) feta cheese, crumbled

2 tablespoons chopped parsley

grated zest of ½ unwaxed lemon

saffron rice

Heat 2 tablespoons of the oil in a large frying pan, add the onion and celery and fry over a medium heat for 5–8 minutes until softened, then stir in the garlic and fry for 3 minutes until softened. Transfer the mixture to the slow cooker.

Heat the remaining oil in the pan, add the aubergine chunks, in batches, and cook over a medium heat for a few minutes on each side until golden. Add to the slow cooker.

Put the remaining ingredients into the slow cooker, season well with salt and pepper, then mix well. Cover with the lid and cook on low for 6 hours until the sauce is thick and the aubergines soft.

Spoon into serving bowls, then sprinkle over the toasted pine nuts, feta, parsley and lemon zest. Serve with saffron rice, or couscous or any other grain to soak up all the delicious juices, or with crusty bread and salad.

These beautiful acorn squash look elegant and impressive when brought to the table. Packed with rice flavoured with herbs and spices and topped with pomegranate molasses, if liked, they make a substantial main meal.

SERVES 2 • PREPARATION TIME 15 MINUTES • COOKING TIME 7 HOURS

STUFFED ACORN SQUASH WITH JEWELLED WILD RICE

200 g (7 oz) cooked wild rice

40 g (1½ oz) dried cranberries

3 spring onions, chopped

40 g (1½ oz) pine nuts

2 tablespoons chopped parsley, plus extra to garnish

2 tablespoons chopped mint leaves, plus extra to garnish

2 tablespoons olive oil

1 acorn squash (or 1 butternut squash with top and bottom removed), halved horizontally and deseeded

1 teaspoon ras el hanout

salt and pepper

pomegranate molasses, to serve (optional)

Mix together the cooked rice, cranberries, spring onions, pine nuts and chopped herbs in a bowl. Add 1 tablespoon of the oil and season well with salt and pepper.

Drizzle the remaining oil over the squash halves and sprinkle over the ras el hanout, then rub the spice and oil all over the flesh using your hands. Season well, then spoon the rice mixture into the centre of each squash half.

Place 2 cooker cutters in the bottom of the slow cooker pot to create trivets (alternatively you can make trivets out of scrunched up foil), then carefully lower the squash halves on top of each trivet so they don't topple over. Cover with the lid and cook on low for 7 hours until the squash is tender.

Serve sprinkled with a little more chopped parsley and mint and drizzled with a little pomegranate molasses, if liked.

A pastilla is a fragrant, spiced pie originating from North Africa. Traditionally filled with meat, this spiral-shaped sweet potato version is packed full of flavour and is perfect for lunch or as a main evening meal.

SERVES 6 • PREPARATION TIME 1½ HOURS, PLUS COOLING • COOKING TIME 2 HOURS

MOROCCAN SPICED SWEET POTATO PASTILLA

4 sweet potatoes, about 750 g (1½ lb) in total, peeled and chopped

2 tablespoons olive oil

2 teaspoons cumin seeds

1 red onion, sliced

1 red, orange or yellow pepper, cored, deseeded and sliced

2 garlic cloves, crushed

1 teaspoon ground cinnamon

1 teaspoon smoked paprika

200 g (7 oz) brown basmati rice

100 g (3½ oz) raisins

1 litre (1¾ pints) vegetable stock

100 g (3½ oz) fresh baby spinach leaves

2 tablespoons chopped parsley

4 sheets filo pastry, plus extra if needed

75 g (3 oz) butter, melted

1 tablespoon poppy seeds

salt and pepper

Preheat the oven to 180°C (350°F), Gas Mark 4. Put the sweet potatoes on a baking tray and drizzle with 1 tablespoon of the olive oil, then sprinkle with the cumin seeds and season with salt and pepper. Toss until well coated. Roast for 30 minutes until tender and golden.

Meanwhile, heat the remaining oil in a large frying pan, add the onion, sliced pepper and a pinch of salt and fry over a medium heat for 5 minutes until softened. Stir in the garlic, cinnamon and paprika and fry for a few minutes until fragrant.

Transfer the onion mixture to the slow cooker and add the roasted sweet potatoes, the rice, raisins and stock. Stir together and season. Cover with the lid and cook on high for 2 hours until the rice is just tender and the liquid has been absorbed to create a soft and thick filling.

Turn off the slow cooker, then stir in the spinach. Replace the lid and leave it to wilt in the residual heat. Carefully transfer the mixture to a bowl and leave to cool completely. Stir in the parsley and adjust the seasoning to taste. Preheat the oven to 190°C (375°F), Gas Mark 5 and place a large baking tray in the oven to warm up.

Place a large piece of baking paper on the work surface. Lay the filo sheets on top to create a large rectangle, with one long and one short edge of each filo sheet overlapping, to create a thicker 'seam'

HARISSA YOGURT

100 ml (3½ fl oz) natural yogurt
2 tablespoons rose harissa
1 tablespoon olive oil

(about 3.5 cm/ 1½ inches wide) along the middle. Brush some of the melted butter to seal the seams. Spoon the cooled filling along the length of the seam to create a long sausage shape, leaving 2.5 cm (1 inch) of pastry at the short edges to avoid the filling spilling out. Brush more butter over the uncovered pastry either side of the sausage shape. With a long edge facing you, fold the pastry nearest you over the filling and tuck it in, then brush the pastry with more butter and roll the sausage shape over itself on to the remaining filo to seal and create a long sausage shape of filling enclosed in pastry. Brush all down the length of the pastry with butter, then carefully curl into a spiral (if the pastry splits, seal up the tears with extra filo pastry and brush with more butter). Tuck under the ends of the spiral, then brush the top with more butter and sprinkle with the poppy seeds.

Carefully lift the pastilla on its baking paper on to the preheated baking tray, then return to the oven and cook for 30–40 minutes until golden brown and crisp on top. Remove the pastilla from the oven and leave to stand for 5–10 minutes. Meanwhile, put all the harissa yogurt ingredients into a bowl and mix together. Serve the pastilla with the harissa yogurt, and maybe a salad for lunch, or with potatoes and steamed vegetables for a main evening meal.

This classic recipe is perfect for entertaining – grilling the aubergine slices means they won't be soggy in the dish. They add great flavour.

SERVES 4 • PREPARATION TIME 1 HOUR • COOKING TIME 7 HOURS

AUBERGINE MOUSSAKA

2 large aubergines, thinly sliced

3 courgettes, thinly sliced

2 tablespoons olive oil, plus extra for brushing and greasing

1 onion, sliced

3 garlic cloves, crushed

200 ml (7 fl oz) red wine

750 g (1½ lb) passata (sieved tomatoes)

400 g (13 oz) can green lentils, drained and rinsed

1 teaspoon dried oregano

2 tablespoons chopped parsley, plus extra to garnish

2 floury potatoes (such as Maris Piper), peeled and thinly sliced

50 g (2 oz) butter

50 g (2 oz) plain flour

500 ml (17 fl oz) milk

good grating of nutmeg

1 large egg, beaten

100 g (3½ oz) feta cheese

salt and pepper

fresh green salad, to serve

Preheat the grill. Brush each side of the aubergine and courgette slices with a little oil, then arrange them in a single layer on a wire rack set in a grill pan. Cook under the grill for 3–5 minutes on each side until tender, then set aside. Repeat until all the slices are cooked.

Meanwhile, heat the oil in a saucepan, add the onion and fry over a medium-low heat for 5 minutes until soft. Stir in the garlic and fry for a few minutes until softened. Pour in the wine, bring to the boil, then bubble until reduced by half. Add the passata, lentils, oregano and parsley. Season well with salt and pepper and simmer for 10 minutes.

Grease the slow cooker pot well with oil. Arrange one-third of the aubergine slices in an even layer in the pot, then add one-third of the courgette slices and one-third of the potato slices. Pour over one-third of the tomato sauce. Repeat until all the vegetables and sauce are used. Cover with the lid and cook on low for 6 hours.

About 15 minutes before the vegetables are cooked, melt the butter in a saucepan over a medium heat. Add the flour and stir together until it resembles a sandy-coloured paste. Cook for a few minutes until it begins to smell biscuity, then pour in some of the milk, remove the pan from the heat and whisk until smooth. Return the pan to the heat and continue to add the milk in small amounts, whisking until smooth after each addition, until all the milk has been added. Simmer for 5 minutes until the sauce is smooth and thick. Season and add the nutmeg. Leave to cool for 5 minutes, then beat in the egg.

Pour the sauce over the the vegetables, then crumble over the feta. Replace the lid and cook for 1 hour until the sauce has set. Garnish with chopped parsley before serving with a fresh green salad.

The peanut butter in this curry adds sweetness and an aromatic nutty flavour similar to a satay sauce. Cooking the rice in coconut milk is a great way to add flavour easily.

SERVES 4 • PREPARATION TIME 20 MINUTES • COOKING TIME 4 HOURS

THAI PEANUT TOFU CURRY

2 tablespoons coconut oil

1 onion, chopped

2 garlic cloves, chopped

1 red chilli, deseeded, if liked, and finely chopped

2 teaspoons garam masala

1 teaspoon turmeric

150 g (5 oz) smooth peanut butter

1 teaspoon tamarind paste

1 sweet potato, peeled and cubed

275 g (9 oz) firm tofu, cubed

400 ml (14 fl oz) can coconut milk

250 ml (8 fl oz) vegetable stock

150 g (5 oz) baby corn

handful of Thai basil, chopped, plus extra to garnish

50 g (2 oz) roasted and salted peanuts, chopped

COCONUT RICE

300 g (10 oz) brown rice

175 ml (6 fl oz) canned coconut milk

175 ml (6 fl oz) vegetable stock

salt and pepper

2 limes, cut into wedges, to serve

Heat the coconut oil in a large frying pan, add the onion and fry over a medium-low heat for 5 minutes until soft and translucent, then stir in the garlic, chilli, garam masala and turmeric and fry for a few minutes until fragrant.

Transfer the onion mixture to the slow cooker, add the peanut butter, tamarind paste, sweet potato, tofu, coconut milk and stock and mix well. Cover with the lid and cook on low for 3 hours 50 minutes. Stir in the corn, replace the lid and cook, still on high, for a further 10 minutes until the sauce is thickened and the vegetables are tender.

Cook the coconut rice about 30 minutes before the end of the curry cooking time. Put all the ingredients into a large saucepan with a lid and bring to the boil. Cover with the lid, then reduce the heat and simmer for about 10 minutes until the rice is tender and the liquid has been absorbed. Remove the pan from the heat and uncover, then place 2 sheets of kitchen paper on top of the pan. Replace the lid and leave to stand for 10 minutes, then fluff up with a fork and season with salt and pepper.

Season the curry to taste and stir through the Thai basil. Divide the rice among 4 serving bowls, then spoon over the curry and top with the chopped peanuts. Garnish with extra Thai basil leaves and serve with the lime wedges for squeezing over.

This tagine is wonderfully spiced and sweet from the dried apricots. The crispy cauliflower leaves add texture and the dish is served topped with toasted flaked almonds.

SERVES 6 · PREPARATION TIME 40 MINUTES · COOKING TIME 4 HOURS

CAULIFLOWER, CHICKPEA & APRICOT TAGINE

1 whole cauliflower

2 tablespoons olive oil

1 teaspoon cumin seeds

2 onions, sliced

4 garlic cloves, crushed

1 teaspoon ras el hanout

1 teaspoon ground cinnamon

1 teaspoon ground coriander

400 g (13 oz) can chopped tomatoes

1 teaspoon tomato purée

400 g (13 oz) can chickpeas, drained

125 g (4 oz) ready-to-eat dried apricots, chopped

10 green olives, pitted and halved

grated zest of ½ unwaxed lemon

400 ml (14 fl oz) water

100 g (3½ oz) fresh spinach leaves

salt and pepper

TO SERVE
handful of coriander, chopped
handful of toasted flaked almonds
herbed couscous

Preheat the oven to 190°C (375°F), Gas Mark 5. Cut the cauliflower into florets, reserving the outer leaves. Put the florets and leaves on a baking sheet and drizzle over 1 tablespoon of the olive oil, then sprinkle with the cumin seeds and season with salt and pepper. Roast for 15 minutes, then remove the leaves and set aside. Return the florets to the oven and continue to cook for 15 minutes until roasted and lightly golden. Set aside.

Meanwhile, heat the remaining oil in a large frying pan, add the onions and a pinch of salt and fry over a medium-low heat for 5 minutes until softened and lightly golden. Stir in the garlic and dried spices and fry for a few minutes until fragrant.

Transfer the onion mixture to the slow cooker and add the chopped tomatoes, tomato purée, chickpeas, apricots, olives and lemon zest. Pour in the measured water, then mix together.

Cover with a lid and cook on low for 4 hours until the sauce is thickened and the vegetables are tender, adding the cauliflower florets (reserving the leaves) 30 minutes before the end of the cooking time.

Turn off the slow cooker, then stir in the spinach. Replace the lid and leave to wilt in the residual heat.

Season to taste, then sprinkle with the coriander and almonds before serving with the roasted cauliflower leaves and herbed couscous.

Beetroot works brilliantly in this Sri Lankan curry, providing sweetness and earthiness while colouring the dish a fantastic pink-red.

SERVES 4 • PREPARATION TIME 20 MINUTES • COOKING TIME 4 HOURS

SRI LANKAN BEETROOT CURRY

3 tablespoons rapeseed oil

6 curry leaves

1 teaspoon mustard seeds

1 teaspoon cumin seeds

1 onion, finely sliced

4 garlic cloves, crushed

1 green chilli, deseeded and
    finely chopped

1 tablespoon tomato purée

650 g (1 lb 7 oz) fresh beetroot,
    peeled and cut into wedges

300 ml (½ pint) water

1 teaspoon salt

400 ml (14 fl oz) can coconut
    milk

TO SERVE

cooked basmati rice

naan breads

natural yogurt with a little
    chopped mint stirred through

Heat the oil in a frying pan until hot, add the curry leaves and fry for 1 minute until they sizzle. Stir in the mustard seeds and cumin seeds and fry for 1–2 minutes until they begin to pop, then reduce the heat to medium-low, add the onion, garlic and chilli and fry for about 5 minutes until the onion has softened.

Transfer the onion mixture to the slow cooker, add the tomato purée, beetroot, measured water and salt and mix well. Cover with the lid and cook on high for 2 hours.

Stir in the coconut milk, replace the lid and cook, still on high, for a further 2 hours until the sauce has thickened and the beetroot is tender.

Serve with fluffy basmati rice, naan breads and cool mint yogurt.

For this recipe you can prepare the eggs up to 4 days in advance – the longer you marinate them, the greater the depth of flavour.

**SERVES 4 · PREPARATION TIME 35 MINUTES, PLUS MARINATING
COOKING TIME 4 HOURS 5 MINUTES**

GINGER & LEMON GRASS PHO

2 cloves

2 cinnamon sticks

2 star anise

1 onion, peeled and cut into quarters

2 garlic cloves, peeled

2.5 cm (1 inch) piece of fresh root ginger, peeled and halved

1 lemon grass stick, bashed and tough outer leaves removed

2.75 litres (5 pints) vegetable stock

2 tablespoons soy sauce

275 g (9 oz) firm tofu, cut into 3.5 cm (1½ inch) cubes

2 baby pak choi, halved lengthways

250 g (8 oz) soba noodles

1 tablespoon sesame oil

25 g (1 oz) shiitake mushrooms, sliced

1 teaspoon sesame seeds

SOY-MARINATED EGGS

2 eggs

150 ml (¼ pint) soy sauce

50 ml (2 fl oz) mirin

TO SERVE

a few mint and coriander sprigs

1 red chilli, sliced

lime wedges

Start by making the marinated eggs. Bring a large saucepan of water to a light simmer and prepare a bowl of iced water alongside. Carefully lower each egg into the simmering water with a slotted spoon, then cook them for 7 minutes. Remove the eggs with the spoon and transfer immediately to the iced water. Leave until completely cold – this will take about 10 minutes. Mix together the soy and mirin in a small bowl. Carefully peel the eggs, then place in the bowl so they are covered in the marinade. Place in an airtight container and leave to marinate in the refrigerator for up to 4 days.

Heat a frying pan over a medium heat, add the cloves, cinnamon and star anise and dry-fry for a few minutes until fragrant and toasted. Tip into the slow cooker. Add the onion, garlic, ginger and lemon grass to the pan and toast for a few minutes until slightly charred. Tip into the slow cooker. Pour in the stock and soy sauce and mix. Cover with the lid. Cook on high for 4 hours until the pho broth is fragrant.

Carefully remove the slow cooker pot from the cooker using oven gloves. Strain the liquid into a bowl, then pour the strained broth back into the pot. Return to the slow cooker. Add the tofu and pak choi, cover with the lid and cook on high for a further 5 minutes.

Meanwhile, cook the noodles according to the packet instructions. Heat the sesame oil in a frying pan, add the shiitake mushrooms and sesame seeds and fry over a medium heat for 5 minutes until golden.

When ready to serve, remove the eggs from the marinade. Divide the noodles between 4 serving bowls, add the pak choi and tofu and ladle over the broth. Top each with half a marinated egg, some mushrooms, fresh herbs and chilli slices. Serve with lime wedges.

1 tablespoon coconut oil

1 onion, chopped

4 garlic cloves, chopped

2 teaspoons garam masala

1 teaspoon curry powder

2 teaspoons turmeric

1 teaspoon ground cumin

2 x 400 ml (14 fl oz) cans coconut milk

2 x 400 g (13 oz) cans chickpeas, drained and rinsed

1 sweet potato, peeled and chopped

1 red pepper, cored, deseeded and thinly sliced

100 g (3½ oz) desiccated coconut

1 large ripe mango, peeled and sliced

salt and pepper

CAULIFLOWER RICE

1 cauliflower, cut into florets

1 tablespoon coconut oil

½ onion, finely chopped

1 teaspoon cumin seeds

TO SERVE

½ red chilli, cut into circles

small handful of coriander leaves

2 limes, cut into wedges

Mango adds sweetness to this lightly spiced coconut curry. The cauliflower rice is very easy to make and is much lighter and healthier than traditional rice.

SERVES 4 • PREPARATION TIME 20 MINUTES COOKING TIME 4 HOURS

CHICKPEA, MANGO & COCONUT CURRY

Heat the coconut oil in a large frying pan, add the onion and fry over a medium-low heat for 5 minutes until soft and translucent. Stir in the garlic and dried spices and fry for a few minutes until fragrant.

Transfer the onion mixture to the slow cooker, add the coconut milk, chickpeas, sweet potato and red pepper and mix together. Cover with the lid and cook on high for 4 hours, stirring occasionally, until the sauce is thick and creamy and the vegetables tender.

Meanwhile, heat a frying pan and add the desiccated coconut. Dry fry over a medium heat for a few minutes, tossing the coconut flakes to make sure they are evenly toasted, until golden. Set aside.

Cook the cauliflower rice about 15 minutes before the end of the curry cooking time. Put the cauliflower into a food processor and pulse until the mixture resembles couscous or breadcrumbs. Heat the coconut oil in a large frying pan, add the onion and fry over a medium-low heat for 5 minutes until soft and translucent. Add the cumin seeds and fry for a further few minutes until they begin to pop and smell fragrant. Tip in the cauliflower, increase the heat to high and fry for about 3–5 minutes until cooked but not too soft. Season well with salt and pepper, then transfer to a serving bowl.

Season the curry to taste, then add the mango and stir through. Serve with the cauliflower rice, topped with the toasted coconut, sliced chilli, coriander leaves and lime wedges.

These beautifully spiced and fragrant curried potatoes really enhance the humble potato. Serve these alongside your favourite curry for a crowd-pleasing potato side dish.

SERVES 4 • PREPARATION TIME 20 MINUTES • COOKING TIME 5 HOURS

BOMBAY SPICED POTATOES

2 tablespoons sunflower oil

1 teaspoon black mustard seeds

1 teaspoon cumin seeds

1 onion, thinly sliced

1 teaspoon garam masala

1 teaspoon curry powder

½ teaspoon dried chilli flakes

1 teaspoon turmeric

400 g (13 oz) can chopped tomatoes

875 g (1¾ lb) potatoes, peeled and cut into 2.5 cm (1 inch) cubes

salt and pepper

handful of coriander, chopped, to garnish

Heat the oil in a large frying pan until hot, add the mustard seeds and cumin seeds and fry for 1–2 minutes until they sizzle and begin to pop. Reduce the heat to medium-low, then add the onion and fry for 5 minutes until soft and translucent. Stir in the remaining dried spices and cook for a further 1 minute until fragrant.

Transfer the onion mixture to the slow cooker, add the chopped tomatoes and potatoes and mix together until well combined. Cover with the lid and cook on low for 5 hours until the sauce has reduced and the potatoes are tender. Season to taste with salt and pepper.

Serve sprinkled with the chopped coriander.

2 red Thai chillies, deseeded and
    chopped
1 thumb-sized piece of fresh root
    ginger, peeled and chopped
4 garlic cloves, chopped
1 teaspoon curry powder
4 small shallots, chopped
1 lemon grass stick, tough outer
    leaves removed and stalk
    chopped
10 g (¼ oz) coriander, leaves and
    stalks separated
1 teaspoon smooth peanut butter
400 ml (14 fl oz) can coconut
    milk
1 litre (1¾ pints) vegetable stock
1 carrot, chopped
½ butternut squash, peeled,
    deseeded and chopped into
    3 cm (1¼ in) cubes (you want
    about 100 g /3½ oz squash)
300 g (10 oz) mangetout
4 baby pak choi, halved
    lengthways
400 g (13 oz) rice noodles
200 g (7 oz) smoked tofu, cubed

TO SERVE
¼ cucumber, cut into long, thin
    strips
handful of bean sprouts
black sesame seeds
lime wedges

A laksa is a fragrant, spiced noodle soup originating from Southeast Asia. A delicious laksa paste is made first and then slow-cooked with the root vegetables and coconut milk to infuse all the flavours. Served with smoked tofu, rice noodles and fresh vegetables, it makes a bright and fragrant dinner.

**SERVES 4 • PREPARATION TIME 25 MINUTES
COOKING TIME 5 HOURS 10 MINUTES**

SMOKED TOFU LAKSA

Put the chillies, ginger, garlic, curry powder, shallots, lemon grass, coriander stalks and peanut butter into a food processor and process to form a smooth paste.

Transfer the paste to the slow cooker, then pour in the coconut milk and stock and add the carrot and squash. Stir, cover with the lid and cook on low for 5 hours until the vegetables are tender.

Turn off the slow cooker and leave to cool slightly, then whizz the soup while still in the slow cooker pot using a stick blender. Alternatively, carefully transfer the soup to a blender and blend, in batches if necessary, until smooth.

Return the soup to the slow cooker, add the mange tout and pak choi, replace the lid and cook on high for 10 minutes until tender.

Meanwhile, cook the rice noodles according to the packet instructions, then drain and set aside.

To serve, stir the smoked tofu pieces through the soup. Divide the rice noodles among 4 serving bowls, then ladle over the laksa soup and tofu. Top with the cucumber strips and bean sprouts. Sprinkle over the black sesame seeds and serve with lime wedges for squeezing over.

SWEET
TREATS

This creamy rice pudding has a gentle aromatic flavour from the cardamom and is incredibly comforting. It is delicious served on its own or with warm stewed fruit.

SERVES 6 • PREPARATION TIME 5 MINUTES • COOKING TIME 4 HOURS

CARDAMOM RICE PUDDING

5 cardamom pods
150 g (5 oz) pudding rice
1 litre (1¾ pints) milk
   or dairy-free milk, such
   as almond or oat
60 g (2¼ oz) demerara sugar
1 cinnamon stick
½ teaspoon ground nutmeg
½ teaspoon vanilla bean paste

Crush the cardamom pods lightly using a pestle and mortar, then remove the skins. Crush the seeds to a fine powder, then transfer to the slow cooker.

Add the remaining ingredients, cover with the lid and cook on low for 4 hours until the rice is tender, creamy and most of the liquid has been absorbed. Remove the cinnamon stick before serving.

Serve warm on its own, or try it with Fruit Compote (see page 17), Pomegranate & Star Anise Poached Pears (see page 112) or fresh fruit, such as berries or mango.

Ricotta makes this simple cheesecake filling not too sweet, making it perfect served with the ginger caramel and orange segments.

SERVES 6 • PREPARATION TIME 25 MINUTES, PLUS COOLING • COOKING TIME 2½ HOURS

GINGER & ORANGE CHEESECAKE

100 g (3½ oz) butter, melted, plus extra for greasing
200 g (7 oz) gingernut biscuits
400 g (13 oz) ricotta cheese
200 g (7 oz) cream cheese
3 large eggs
2 tablespoons plain flour
150 g (5 oz) caster sugar
grated zest of 1 orange, plus 2 tablespoons orange juice
½ teaspoon vanilla extract
1 orange, pith removed and cut into segments, to decorate

50 g (2 oz) caster sugar
20 g (¾ oz) unsalted butter
125 ml (4 fl oz) double cream
60 g (2¼ oz) stem ginger, finely chopped
3 tablespoons syrup from the stem ginger jar

Grease the bottom of a 17 cm (6½ inch) springform cake tin with butter and line with baking paper.

Put the biscuits into a food processor and process until they form fine crumbs. Add the melted butter and process until the mixture resembles wet sand. Alternatively, put the biscuits into a plastic food bag and tap lightly with a rolling pin until crushed, then tip into a bowl and mix in the melted butter. Tip the mixture into the prepared cake tin and press firmly into the bottom. Place in the refrigerator.

Put the cheeses, eggs, flour, sugar, orange zest and juice and vanilla into a large bowl and beat together until smooth and well combined. Remove the biscuit base from the refrigerator and pour in the filling.

Place a cookie cutter or upturned heatproof bowl in the bottom of the slow cooker pot to create a trivet. Pour in boiling water to about 1.5 cm (¾ inch) high, ensuring the base of the tin will not touch the water, then carefully lower the tin on top of the trivet. Cover with the lid and cook on high for 2½ hours until firm and set. Turn off the cooker and, with the lid on, leave the cheesecake to cool for 2 hours.

When ready to serve, make the caramel. Heat the sugar in a heavy-based saucepan over a medium heat until dissolved, then bubble for about 10 minutes until golden brown (you want a fairly dark caramel). Remove the pan from the heat and carefully stir in the butter. Pour in the cream and whisk until smooth, then add the stem ginger and syrup and whisk again until smooth. Leave to cool slightly.

Remove the cheesecake from the slow cooker, then run a knife gently around the edge of the tin before releasing. Decorate with the orange segments and serve drizzled with the caramel sauce.

These poached pears are delicious and so simple to prepare. They look impressive as the whole pears are suffused with the beautiful deep wine colour.

SERVES 4 · PREPARATION TIME 15 MINUTES · COOKING TIME 3 HOURS

POMEGRANATE & STAR ANISE POACHED PEARS

4 firm, ripe pears

600 ml (1 pint) pomegranate juice

400 ml (14 fl oz) red wine

1 tablespoon pomegranate molasses

1 cinnamon stick

2 star anise

1 teaspoon vanilla bean paste or 1 vanilla pod

1 tablespoon caster sugar

toasted chopped nuts or fresh pomegranate seeds, to serve

Peel the pears, keeping them whole and retaining the stalks. Put into the slow cooker and add the remaining ingredients. Cover with the lid and cook on low for 3 hours until the pears are cooked through and tender.

Carefully remove the slow cooker pot from the cooker using oven gloves, then remove the pears with a slotted spoon and set aside. Remove the cinnamon stick, star anise and vanilla pod, if using. Carefully pour the cooking liquid into a small saucepan and simmer for about 10 minutes until reduced and syrupy.

Drizzle the poached pears with the syrup and top with toasted chopped nuts or fresh pomegranate seeds. You can eat them by themselves, or serve with ice cream, crème fraîche, yogurt or Cardamom Rice Pudding (see page 110).

This bread and butter pudding is made extra special with the use of buttery brioche bread, and is flavoured with orange, dried fig and cinnamon. Adding orange zest lifts traditional custard to another level and works perfectly paired with this dessert.

SERVES 4 • PREPARATION TIME 10 MINUTES • COOKING TIME 3 HOURS

FIG & CINNAMON BRIOCHE BREAD & BUTTER PUDDING

4 eggs
500 ml (17 fl oz) milk
50 g (2 oz) caster sugar
1 teaspoon ground cinnamon
½ teaspoon ground nutmeg
1 teaspoon vanilla bean paste
grated zest of 1 orange
625 g (1¼ lb) brioche loaf, cut into large cubes
150 g (5 oz) soft dried figs, chopped
butter, for greasing

ORANGE CUSTARD
500 g (1 lb) vanilla custard
grated zest of 1 orange

Put the eggs, milk, sugar, spices, vanilla bean paste and orange zest into a large bowl and whisk until well combined. Add the brioche and dried figs and toss in the egg mixture until well coated.

Grease the slow cooker pot with butter, then add the brioche mixture, pouring in all the egg. Cover with the lid and cook on low for 3 hours until the custard is set.

When ready to serve, make the orange custard. Heat the vanilla custard according to the packet instructions and stir through the grated orange zest.

Serve the bread and butter pudding with the orange custard.

The combination of coconut and lime in this pudding gives a Caribbean twist and flavour. There is a delicious sweet sauce at the base that can be spooned over the sponge when serving.

SERVES 6 • PREPARATION TIME 20 MINUTES • COOKING TIME 2 HOURS

LEMON, LIME & COCONUT SELF-SAUCING PUDDING

100 g (3½ oz) butter, softened, plus extra for greasing

150 g (5 oz) caster sugar

4 eggs, separated

150 ml (¼ pint) milk

400 ml (14 fl oz) can coconut milk

grated zest and juice of 1 unwaxed lemon

grated zest and juice of 1 unwaxed lime

75 g (3 oz) self-raising flour, sifted

icing sugar, for dusting

Use a hand-held electric whisk to beat together the butter, sugar and egg yolks in a large bowl for about 5 minutes until pale, fluffy and voluminous. With the electric whisk still running, drizzle in the milk and coconut milk and continue to beat until combined. Add the citrus zest and juice and the flour and carefully fold in until combined.

Whisk the egg whites in a separate clean bowl using clean beaters until medium peaks form. Gently fold a large spoonful of the whites into the cake batter to loosen the mixture, then carefully fold in the remaining whites until just combined, taking care not to overmix and knock the air out.

Grease the slow cooker pot well with butter, then add the batter, top with a clean tea towel and cover with the lid. Cook on high for 2 hours until the sponge is set on the top with a custardy layer of sauce underneath.

Dust with icing sugar and serve immediately. Try it with ice cream, crème fraîche or fresh berries, if liked.

A classic banana and walnut bread recipe that is brilliant for afternoon tea or for breakfast. Cooking it in the slow cooker keeps the bread very moist and stops it from drying out.

MAKES 10 SLICES • PREPARATION TIME 25 MINUTES • COOKING TIME 2 HOURS

BANANA & WALNUT BREAD

75 g (3 oz) unsalted butter, softened, plus extra for greasing
100 g (3½ oz) soft brown sugar
2 large eggs, lightly beaten
3 ripe bananas, mashed, plus 1 less ripe banana, halved lengthways, to decorate (optional)
1 teaspoon vanilla extract
225 g (7½ oz) plain flour
2 teaspoons baking powder
¼ teaspoon bicarbonate of soda
½ teaspoon fine salt
½ teaspoon ground cinnamon
½ teaspoon ground nutmeg
75 g (3 oz) walnuts, roughly chopped

Grease the bottom of a 900 g (2 lb) loaf tin. Cut a long strip of baking paper to fit the length and slightly above the short sides of the tin, then use to line the tin (this makes it easier to remove the bread from the tin once baked).

Beat together the butter and sugar in a large bowl using a hand-held electric whisk until light and fluffy. Add the eggs, mashed bananas and vanilla extract and beat again until smooth and well combined.

Mix together the dry ingredients and two-thirds of the walnuts in a separate bowl, then fold into the banana mixture until the dry ingredients are well incorporated and there are no floury pockets.

Spoon the batter into the prepared loaf tin and smooth the top. Gently press the halved banana pieces, if using, into the batter, cut sides up, and sprinkle with the remaining walnuts.

Lower the tin into the slow cooker, then cover with the lid and cook on high for 2 hours, or until a metal skewer inserted into the middle of the bread comes out clean.

Carefully remove the tin from the slow cooker using oven gloves and leave the banana bread to cool in the tin. Remove using the baking paper tabs, then serve cut into slices.

This rich and decadent cake calls for Armagnac-soaked prunes, which add a delicious boozy kick. The result is rich and chocolatey.

**SERVES 6 • PREPARATION TIME 20 MINUTES, PLUS SOAKING
COOKING TIME 1½ HOURS**

DARK CHOCOLATE, PRUNE & ARMAGNAC CAKE

200 g (7 oz) soft prunes, roughly chopped
50 ml (2 fl oz) Armagnac
2 teaspoons vanilla extract
200 g (7 oz) plain dark chocolate, broken into pieces
100 g (3½ oz) unsalted butter, plus extra for greasing
4 large eggs
200 g (7 oz) caster sugar
½ teaspoon fine salt
100 g (3½ oz) ground almonds
50 g (2 oz) plain flour

TO SERVE
cocoa powder
crème fraîche

Put the prunes into a shallow dish, then pour over the Armagnac and vanilla extract and leave to soak for a minimum of 2 hours or preferably overnight.

Melt the chocolate and butter in a heatproof bowl set over a saucepan of gently simmering water, ensuring the bottom of the bowl does not touch the water. Remove from the heat and leave to cool slightly.

Grease a 20 cm (8 inch) springform cake tin with butter and line with baking paper. Seal around the outside bottom edge with foil.

Whisk together the eggs, sugar and salt in a large bowl until pale and fluffy, then carefully fold in the melted chocolate and soaked prunes, including the liquid. Fold in the ground almonds and flour, taking care not to overmix and knock the air out. Pour the batter into the prepared cake tin.

Lower the tin into the slow cooker, then carefully pour boiling water into the pot to come about halfway up the side of the tin. Cover with the lid and cook on high for 1½ hours until the cake is set but still has a slight wobble in the middle.

Carefully remove the tin from the slow cooker using oven gloves and transfer to a wire rack to cool the cake completely, then remove from the tin and serve cut into slices. Serve dusted with cocoa powder and with dollops of crème fraîche.

A slow cooker is perfect for creating crème brûlée because the temperature is low and controlled, and creating a water bath cooks these Earl Grey-flavoured custards really gently. Finished with the classic sugar brûlée crust, these make an impressive and delicious dessert.

SERVES 2 • PREPARATION TIME 20 MINUTES, PLUS STANDING & COOLING COOKING TIME 2 HOURS

EARL GREY CREME BRULEE

400 ml (14 fl oz) double cream
100 ml (3½ fl oz) milk
1 tablespoon vanilla bean paste
2 Earl Grey tea bags
3 large egg yolks
75 g (3 oz) caster sugar, plus
   2 tablespoons for the crust

Put the cream, milk, vanilla and tea bags into a saucepan and warm over a medium heat until just below boiling point, then remove from the heat, cover with a lid and leave to stand for 10 minutes.

Whisk together the egg yolks and sugar in a large heatproof bowl until pale and fluffy. Remove the teabags from the milk mixture, then slowly pour over the egg yolks, whisking continuously. Pour the mixture into 2 x 9 cm (3½ inch) ramekins.

Lower the ramekins into the slow cooker, then carefully pour boiling water into the pot to come about halfway up the sides of the dishes. Cover with the lid and cook on low for 2 hours until the custard is set.

Carefully remove the ramekins from the slow cooker using a clean tea towel and transfer to a wire rack to cool. When cool enough to handle, transfer to the refrigerator and leave to cool completely for 1–2 hours or chill overnight.

When ready to serve, sprinkle a tablespoon of sugar in an even layer over each ramekin, tapping off any excess. Heat the tops using a kitchen blowtorch until the sugar is crisp and caramelized. Alternatively, place the ramekins under a preheated grill for 2 minutes until caramelized. Leave the sugar to cool and harden for a couple of minutes before serving.

Slow cooking is the perfect method for cooking and steaming this dessert. The almond-based sponge with blackberry compote is a fantastic pairing and is delicious served warm with plenty of custard.

SERVES 4 • PREPARATION TIME 30 MINUTES, PLUS COOLING COOKING TIME 2½ HOURS

BLACKBERRY & ALMOND STEAMED PUDDING

100 g (3½ oz) butter, softened,
   plus extra for greasing
100 g (3½ oz) self-raising flour
100 g (3½ oz) soft brown sugar
2 large eggs
50 g (2 oz) ground almonds
1 teaspoon almond extract
1 tablespoon milk

BLACKBERRY COMPOTE
300 g (10 oz) fresh or frozen
   blackberries
100 g (3½ oz) demerara sugar
100 ml (3½ fl oz) water
1 cinnamon stick

vanilla custard, to serve

Put all the compote ingredients into a saucepan and bubble over a low heat for 10–15 minutes until the blackberries have broken down and the mixture is thickened and jammy. Leave to cool completely, then remove the cinnamon stick.

Grease a 1 litre (1¾ pint), 17 cm (6½ inch) pudding basin generously with butter. To make the sponge, put all the ingredients into a large bowl and beat together until completely combined and smooth.

Spoon the cooled compote into the prepared basin, then spoon in the sponge batter and smooth the top. Cover the basin with a piece of nonstick baking paper that has been folded with a pleat and secure with kitchen string, then cover with foil, ensuring it is well sealed. Wrap another piece of string around the basin and secure to create a string handle.

Lower the basin into the slow cooker, then carefully pour boiling water into the pot to come about halfway up the sides of the dish, under the lip of the pudding basin. Cover with the lid and cook on high for 2½ hours. Turn off the slow cooker and leave the pudding to cool slightly for about 10 minutes.

Carefully remove the pudding from the slow cooker using the string handle, remove the foil and paper, then tip out on to a serving plate. Serve with vanilla custard.

These little chocolate mousses with an espresso hit are a real crowd-pleaser and look like they are far more work than they really are. The chopped pistachios on top give the mousse a lovely crunchy, nutty flavour.

SERVES 4 • PREPARATION TIME 25 MINUTES • COOKING TIME 1 HOUR

CHOCOLATE & ESPRESSO MOUSSE

150 g (5 oz) plain dark
    chocolate, broken into pieces
100 ml (3½ fl oz) freshly made
    strong espresso, cooled
pinch of sea salt
3 large eggs, separated
100 g (3½ oz) caster sugar

TO SERVE
chocolate shavings
handful of chopped pistachio
    nuts

Melt the chocolate in a heatproof bowl set over a saucepan of gently simmering water, ensuring the bottom of the bowl does not touch the water. Remove from the heat and leave to cool slightly, then stir in the espresso and salt.

Whisk together the egg yolks and sugar in a separate bowl with a hand-held electric whisk until pale, fluffy and voluminous. Add the melted chocolate mixture and stir until combined.

Whisk the egg whites in a clean bowl using clean beaters until medium-soft peaks form, then gently fold into the chocolate mixture until combined. Spoon the mousse into 4 x 9 cm (3½ inch) ramekins.

Lower the ramekins into the slow cooker, then carefully pour boiling water into the pot to come about halfway up the sides of the dishes. Cover with the lid and cook on high for 1 hour until just set.

Carefully remove the ramekins from the slow cooker using a clean tea towel and leave to cool slightly. Serve topped with chocolate shavings and a sprinkle of pistachio nuts. You can add a spoonful of whipped cream, if you like.

INDEX

A

artichokes: braised artichokes with mustard vinaigrette 77
aubergines
    aubergine moussaka 96
    Greek aubergine & tomato stew 90
    ratatouille bake with ciabatta crust 73

B

banana & walnut bread 117
beans
    Mexican black bean chilli tacos 89
    smoky breakfast beans 23
    vegetarian sausage & white bean stew 52
beetroot
    beetroot risotto with Stilton & walnuts 29
    Sri Lankan beetroot curry 100
blackberry & almond steamed pudding 123
blueberry & cinnamon French toast 18
bread
    chilli, cheese & chive cornbread 38
    seeded malt bread 74
    tomato & rosemary focaccia 36
broccoli & cauliflower cheese 45
butternut squash, carrot & fennel soup 35

C

cabbage
    braised red cabbage with cider 76
    stuffed cabbage leaves 54
cauliflower
    broccoli & cauliflower cheese 45
    cauliflower, chickpea & apricot tagine 98
celeriac
    lentil & celeriac 'shepherd's pie' 86–7
    potato, fennel & celeriac gratin 46
Cheddar cheese
    broccoli & cauliflower cheese 45
    chilli, cheese & chive cornbread 38
chestnuts: stuffed cabbage leaves 54
chickpeas
    cauliflower, chickpea & apricot tagine 98
    chickpea, mango & coconut curry 104
    Greek aubergine & tomato stew 90
chilli
    chilli, cheese & chive cornbread 38
    Mexican black bean chilli tacos 89
chocolate
    chocolate & espresso mousse 124
    dark chocolate, prune & armagnac cake 119
courgettes: ratatouille bake with ciabatta crust 73
cream: Earl Grey crème brûlée 120
curries
    chickpea, mango & coconut curry 104
    coconut dhal with paneer 57
    sag aloo paneer 60
    Sri Lankan beetroot curry 100
    sweet potato curry with toasted cashews 58
    Thai peanut tofu curry 97
    vegetable biryani 55

E

eggs
    shakshuka 20
    sweet potato, goats' cheese & thyme frittata 19
Emmental cheese
    French onion soup with mustardy Emmental croutons 66
    potato, fennel & celeriac gratin 46

F

feta cheese
    lemony greens & feta filo pie 49
    shakshuka 20
fig & cinnamon brioche bread & butter pudding 114
fruit compote 17

G

goats' cheese
    confit tomato tart 80
    goats' cheese, leek & spinach conchiglie bake 69
    sweet potato, goats' cheese & thyme frittata 19

J

jackfruit: Chinese hoisin pulled jackfruit 63
jam: raspberry chia seed jam 16

L

lemon, lime & coconut self-saucing pudding 115
lentils
    coconut dhal with paneer 57
    lentil & celeriac 'shepherd's pie' 86–7

M

milk: golden turmeric milk 11

mushrooms

creamy wild mushroom stroganoff 84

mushroom bolognese 70

mushroom pearl barley risotto 26

sun-dried tomato & olive-stuffed mushrooms 79

N

noodles

ginger & lemon grass pho 103

smoked tofu laksa 106

O

oats

honey, nut & seed granola 14

slow cooker creamy porridge 10

onions: French onion soup with mustardy Emmental croutons 66

P

paneer

coconut dhal with paneer 57

sag aloo paneer 60

parsnip & apple soup 31

pasta

creamy orzo with green veg 42

goats' cheese, leek & spinach conchiglie bake 69

mac & cheese with leeks & crispy breadcrumb topping 40

mushroom bolognese 70

pumpkin, Brie & sage lasagne 85

spinach & ricotta tortellini bake 44

pearl barley: mushroom pearl barley risotto 26

pears: pomegranate & star anise poached pears 112

peas

pea & watercress soup 32

summery pea, asparagus & lemon risotto 30

peppers: spelt & halloumi stuffed peppers 51

pesto: minestrone soup 68

polenta

chilli, cheese & chive cornbread 38

creamy cheesy polenta 39

potatoes

Bombay spiced potatoes 105

potato, fennel & celeriac gratin 46

sag aloo paneer 60

prunes: dark chocolate, prune & armagnac cake 119

pumpkin, brie & sage lasagne 85

R

raspberry chia seed jam 16

rice. see also curries

beetroot risotto with Stilton & walnuts 29

cardamom rice pudding 110

stuffed acorn squash with jewelled wild rice 93

stuffed cabbage leaves 54

summery pea, asparagus & lemon risotto 30

vegetable biryani 55

S

salsa: Mexican black bean chilli tacos 89

sausages: vegetarian sausage & white bean stew 52

soup

butternut squash, carrot & fennel soup 35

minestrone soup 68

parsnip & apple soup 31

pea & watercress soup 32

spelt & halloumi stuffed peppers 51

spinach

sag aloo paneer 60

spinach & ricotta tortellini bake 44

squash: stuffed acorn squash with jewelled wild rice 93

Stilton cheese: beetroot risotto with Stilton & walnuts 29

sweet potatoes

Moroccan spiced sweet potato pastilla 94–5

sweet potato curry with toasted cashews 58

sweet potato, goats' cheese & thyme frittata 19

T

toast: blueberry & cinnamon French toast 18

tofu

ginger & lemon grass pho 103

smoked tofu laksa 106

Thai peanut tofu curry 97

tomatoes

confit tomato tart 80

shakshuka 20

smoky breakfast beans 23

tomato & rosemary focaccia 36

ultimate slow-cooked tomato sauce 72

turmeric: golden turmeric milk 11

V

vegetables

creamy orzo with green veg 42

lemony greens & feta filo pie 49

root vegetable puff pastry pie 82

vegetable biryani 55

W

walnuts: beetroot risotto with Stilton & walnuts 29

watercress: pea & watercress soup 32

Y

yoghurt: bio-cultured yogurt 13

COOK'S NOTES

aubergine = eggplant

baking beans = pie weights

black beans = turtle beans

borlotti beans = cranberry beans

broad beans = fava beans

beetroot = beet

bicarbonate of soda = baking soda

biscuit = cookie

caster sugar = superfine sugar

celeriac = celery root

chestnut mushrooms = cremini mushrooms

chocolate, plain dark = chocolate, bittersweet

cider = hard cider

clingfilm = plastic wrap

coriander = cilantro

courgette = zucchini

coconut, desiccated = coconut, dried shredded

demerara sugar = turbinado sugar

double cream = heavy cream

fast-action dried yeast = active dry yeast

filo pastry = phyllo pastry

greaseproof paper = wax paper

grill = broiler; to broil

groundnut oil = peanut oil

hand-held electric whisk = hand mixer

haricot beans = navy beans

icing sugar = confectioners' sugar

kitchen paper = paper towels

mangetout = snowpea

pak choi = bok choi

plain flour = all-purpose flour

polenta = cornmeal

pudding basin = ovenproof round bowl

pudding rice = short-grain rice

rapeseed oil = canola oil

rocket = arugula

self-raising flour = self-rising flour

shortcrust pastry = pie dough

spring onions = scallions

stick blender = immersion blender

tea towel = dish towel

tomato pureé = tomato paste

vanilla pod = vanilla bean

vegetable stock = vegetable broth

yogurt, natural = yogurt, plain

Standard level spoon measurements
are used in all recipes.

1 tablespoon = one 15 ml spoon

1 teaspoon = one 5 ml spoon

Both imperial and metric measurements
have been given in all recipes. Use one set
of measurements only and not a mixture
of both.